Sea Power and Strategy in the INDIAN OCEAN

Sea Power and Strategy in the INDIAN OCEAN

ALVIN J. COTTRELL and Associates

Published in cooperation with the
Center for Strategic & International Studies,
Georgetown University

 **SAGE PUBLICATIONS**   Beverly Hills   London

For information address:

SAGE Publications, Inc.
275 South Beverly Drive
Beverly Hills, California 90212

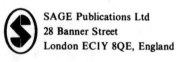

SAGE Publications Ltd
28 Banner Street
London EC1Y 8QE, England

Printed in the United States of America

Library of Congress Cataloging in Publication Data
Main entry under title:

Cottrell, Alvin J
 Sea power and strategy in the Indian Ocean

 Bibliography: p.
 Includes index.
 1. Sea-power—Indian Ocean.   2. Indian Ocean—
Strategic aspects.   3. Naval strategy.   I. Georgetown
University, Washington, D.C. Center for Strategic
and International Studies.   II. Title.
 V25.C67   359'.03'091824   80-28415
 ISBN 0-8039-1577-2   AACR1

FIRST PRINTING

CONTENTS

ACKNOWLEDGMENTS

The authors would like to thank Mr. Walter F. Hahn, editor-in-chief of the *U.S. Strategic Review*, for his assistance on the section involving naval strategy and bases in the Indian Ocean. We are also most grateful to Alexandria Williams of the Fletcher School of Law and Diplomacy, who was a summer research scholar in the CSIS Maritime Policy Studies program, for preparing the index and bibliography and for other editorial assistance in readying the book for publication.

We would also like to express our appreciation to Ilse Muller for helping with typing and editorial aspects involved in readying the book for the publisher. Many of the ideas and views expressed in the following pages were the subject of the Center's first conference under the auspices of its newly formed Executive Directorate of Maritime Policy Studies on April 9, 1980. We are profoundly grateful to all the participants in that conference for their contribution to our thoughts on naval policy and strategy. The authors are solely responsible for the substance of the volume.

Spring 1981

INTRODUCTION

Thomas H. Moorer

The United States is an island nation and has always been primarily a maritime power. By contrast, the Soviet Union has always been a land power with, until recently, far less need to project naval power in defense of its interests. Today, the need for the United States to project a strong naval presence is increasing at a time when its ability to do so is declining, and nowhere is maritime power more important than in the northwest quadrant of the Indian Ocean, the area that includes the Arabian Peninsula, the Persian Gulf, the Arabian Sea, and the Strait of Hormuz.

One of the most significant developments affecting the future of U.S. naval power is the change taking place in the political environment of the landmass in this region, one of the farthest points in the world from the United States. The fall of the Iranian monarchy and its consequent political changes on the Iranian side of the Gulf suggest, as Professor Geoffrey Kemp states, "that a position of maritime superiority could rapidly shift to one of maritime inferiority if control of the landmass were to change." Hence, present U.S. maritime superiority in this vital region could disappear if the Soviet Union were able to secure military facilities on the Arabian Peninsula, in Iran, or in southwestern Pakistan. Such a Soviet advantage would help to offset significantly the present U.S. control of the sea that results from the latter's ability to deploy large attack aircraft carrier task forces to this region.

The importance of the Persian Gulf is brought out succinctly in a chapter by Robert J. Hanks and Alvin J. Cottrell on the Strait of Hormuz, in which they discuss the importance of the area as a critical chokepoint for the West. This 100-mile-long strait, which narrows sharply at the juncture of the Persian Gulf and the Gulf of Oman, is now and will remain for some time to come a vital waterway, vulnerable to both political and military change. The western side is now under the control of the pro-Western Sultan of Oman; and the eastern shore, since 1979, has been under the uncertain control of revolutionary forces in Iran. Admiral Hanks and Dr. Cottrell discuss in detail the potential political and military threats to this region. As they point out, "the greatest threat to the interests of the United States and the other large industrial powers is the political instability of the Persian Gulf region."

All too often we read about the need to protect the sea lines of communication (SLOCs) in the Persian Gulf-Hormuz area. This is indeed a serious problem because of the SLOC's proximity to the littoral. Nowhere along the vital Cape sea route around southern Africa are they more vulnerable; the possibility of political change, such as has occurred in Iran, heightens the danger to the shipping lanes. This vulnerability is due to geography. The Persian Gulf is 600 miles long; it is 185 miles wide at its widest point in the southern Gulf but only 21 miles wide at its narrowest point in the Strait of Hormuz. Thus, political stability is of primary importance for the flow of oil. Militarily, it is clear, as the authors indicate, that potential threats to oil tankers transiting Hormuz are many and varied. Until the Iranian revolution there was very little fear of hostile action against ships in the strait, but now the threat of harassment is a distinct possibility.

The United States must be able to project naval force over long distances in order to protect U.S. interests and the interests of its friends. No great power has ever been located on the littoral of this region—or, indeed, of the entire Indian Ocean—and all real military power has thus far entered the region from the sea, principally British power over the past 150 years and, before that, Dutch and Portuguese.

This volume begins appropriately by discussing the history and philosophical considerations involved in the role of seapower in a chapter by Professor Geoffrey Kemp of the Fletcher School of Law and Diplomacy of Tufts University. His essay focuses on the relationship between maritime power and maritime access, with special reference to the contemporary crisis the world faces over the security of Persian Gulf oil supplies. As he observes, "What is happening as the end of the twentieth century approaches is that Western maritime power is declining at the same time dependency on maritime power is increasing." He believes that, to a large extent, this is relative to other identifiable world developments: the great increase in Soviet naval power, the new law of the sea that will restrict access to world ocean resources, the proliferation of military technology to key states in the less developed world, and the failure of Western industrial states to curtail substantially the importation of oil from the Persian Gulf.

Finally, the book discusses U.S. naval requirements for dealing with the erosion of stability in the area and the protection of regional SLOCs. In a chapter dealing with the Indian Ocean, Dr. Cottrell and I discuss the question of a permanent U.S. naval presence in the Indian Ocean and the naval forces and infrastructure that would be necessary to sustain it. The United States has neglected this area strategically ever since the final British withdrawal east of Suez on November 30, 1971.

Against the backdrop of growing crises in Iran and Afghanistan, the United States has dispatched to the Indian Ocean area two aircraft carrier battle groups, periodically augmented by a detachment of 1500 Marines on afloat station. These deployments are temporary, however, the forces having been borrowed from those on permanent station elsewhere in the world—from the Sixth Fleet in the Mediterranean and the Seventh Fleet in the Pacific. At some point they will have to be returned so that stability in the areas from which they came will not be adversely affected.

Even if the necessary forces can be earmarked and assembled, however, they will need access to a network of forward bases and facilities in the region: ports for servicing naval vessels and their crews, airfields for air operations and for the staging of airlifted fighting units, and sites for the prepositioning of military equipment. These basing facilities are vital for logistical reasons, but there is now additional reason for them. If we do not maintain such an onshore infrastructure, our military credibility will remain low because the basing structure is needed to convince local leaders that our presence is permanent, not just for the duration of a particular crisis. In so many of the previous deployments to the area, such as the *Enterprise* task force during the Indo-Pakistan war of 1971, our ships remained several months and then departed.

Today, the United States has assured access only to its naval and air facilities on the island of Diego Garcia, in the center of the Indian Ocean. But Diego Garcia is more than 2000 miles from the Persian Gulf. Closer facilities will be needed, and we have discussed additional basing requirements in other countries and the policy considerations involved.

The search for the needed additional facilities may already be too late. The United States should have begun such efforts in the early 1970s, after Great Britain withdrew its last forces and when the Arab oil embargo gave a clear indication of possible serious threats to vital U.S. and allied interests. Today, against the background of what is perceived as American irresoluteness and dwindling power in the region, even regional powers basically friendly to the United States, such as Saudi Arabia, are reluctant to incur the political risks that might be involved in any close association with the United States.

The key to U.S. interests in the region is Saudi Arabia. The prime objective of U.S. political and military policy must be to maintain the stability of the Saudi state. Yet Saudi Arabia's faith in the United States has declined to the point where any explicit U.S. military arrangements with that country are highly unlikely. Instead, the Saudis argue, a regional military presence by the United States must be designed precisely to enhance Saudi security and restore firm U.S.-Saudi links.

The opportunities for establishing such a military presence are dwindling rapidly. The trends in the region, from the U.S. perspective, are approaching a point of no return. There is very little time, and there is even less margin for error. We hope we have helped to clarify the issues involved and to emphasize the relationship of maritime power to our most pressing national security problem: continued access to the oil resources of the Persian Gulf.

I. Maritime Access and Maritime Power: The Past, the Persian Gulf, and the Future

Geoffrey Kemp

T his essay focuses on the relationship between maritime power and maritime access, with special reference to the crisis the Western world faces over the security of the Persian Gulf oil supplies. As the end of the twentieth century approaches, Western maritime power is declining at the same time dependency on maritime access is increasing. There are several reasons for this, including the growth of Soviet military power, the laws that will limit access to the world's sea resources, the spread of military technology to key countries in the less developed regions, and the failure of the Western world to make substantial cuts in its consumption of Persian Gulf oil.

None of these trends are decisive or irreversible. However, if the Western maritime countries are to reestablish their predominant power, the magnitude of the issues must be faced. This essay attempts to relate historical trends to the future actions Western countries need to take to avoid catastrophes that would occur if oil supplies were to fall under Soviet control.

The first part of the essay, which looks at historical perspectives, argues that the control of the spice trade in the fourteenth century by the Middle East countries motivated the European maritime powers to embark on the route that led to the Age of Discovery. The second examines the concept of maritime power and the relevance of the writings of Alfred Mahan in understanding the current U.S.-Soviet maritime rivalry. This section also points out some of the deficiencies in Mahan's concepts of sea power: in particular, his downplaying of the role of technology and logistics in determining the relative maritime power of states. The final section deals with the emerging maritime environment and the challenges and promises this poses for Western countries in the years ahead.

HISTORICAL PERSPECTIVES: THE SPICE TRADE AND THE AGE OF DISCOVERY

Ever since the 1973 Arab-Israeli war and the subsequent oil embargo, concern over the supply of strategic war materials has come to the forefront in military planning. For the first time since World War II, the security of overseas strategic resources, particularly those that come from conflict regions in the less industrial world, is in question. The concern is based on three related phenomena: the growing dependency of advanced Western economic powers on the raw materials of the Middle East, Africa, Asia, and Latin America; the relative self-sufficiency of the Soviet Union in most of these same resources; and the diminution of effective Western military power paralleled by the growth of Soviet military capabilities in the regions on which the West is becoming so dependent.

The most obvious example of this is the dependency on oil from the Persian Gulf. However, it is matched in some respects by the European and Japanese dependency on minerals from Southern Africa. As a result of these significant changes, the need has arisen to protect the lines of communication from the sources of the materials to their destinations.

Although this concern is appropriate, in historical terms the problem can be regarded as a short-term phenomenon—serious, perhaps even critical, but short-term nevertheless. The reasons for such optimism result from the assumption that if we can learn anything at all from history, it is that over time all such resource dependencies can be overcome provided there is sufficient political enlightenment and the will to bring about change. For, over time, new sources of raw materials and, therefore, new lines of communication can be established; new technologies can reduce existing dependencies on particular materials; new political alignments may reduce the strategic vulnerability of existing sources.

Historically, the world's seas and waterways have been used to secure access to raw materials and markets. Maritime powers such as the Phoenicians sailed beyond the confines of the ancient world and may even have circumnavigated Africa. It is clear that in the ancient world there was an understanding of the importance of maritime access for economic, political, and military purposes. The major constraint on maritime activity in those days was technical rather than intellectual.

During the heyday of the Roman Empire a flourishing trade developed with the East involving both land and sea routes, of which the Silk Road was perhaps the most famous legacy. Roman, Arab, Persian, Indian, and Chinese merchants made great profits from trade. Following the fall of Rome in the fifth century, the extent of knowledge about the sea was restricted to coastal trade, which flourished in Europe and throughout the Middle East and Asia. Two important exceptions were the exploits of the Vikings, a Nordic race from the cold, harsh climate and terrain of Scandinavia, and the Polynesians, an island people set in the middle of the vast, warm Pacific Ocean.

The Vikings, in particular, provided a remarkable example of the effective exercise of maritime power in order to ensure access to the supplies they needed. Denied easy markets because of their remote geographical position, they had to sail far from their homes in order to survive and develop economically. Although they frequently engaged in terror tactics and plundered the coastal villages of Britain and the Low Countries, they also established an extraordinary pattern of sea and water trade routes reaching across Europe to the Danube. One reason for their achievements was technical: The Vikings had developed a ship capable of sailing much closer to the wind than traditional coastal vessels. It was therefore able to outmaneuver the opposition and sail into the wind. Furthermore, its shallow draft permitted it to sail up shallow rivers and estuaries. Finally, the Vikings established an excellent system of navigation. Although they rarely sailed beyond sight of land they were able to cross the Atlantic with great accuracy and make repeat journeys.

Following the Mongol conquest of Asia in the twelfth century, however, important changes in the patterns of European commerce took place. One effect of the conquest was to reestablish trade links between China and Europe, and by the end of the thirteenth century two routes were in use. The first went from the Crimea, through central Asia and Mongolia to Peking; the other route went from the Black Sea through Persia, Afghanistan, and Sinkiang. In addition to the land communications, which paralleled the old Silk Road, the conquests also opened up the sea route that became known as the spice route. The route went by land from the Black Sea, through Persia to Hormuz at the mouth of the Persian Gulf, and on to India and the Far East. Sailing ships could not regularly make the journey to the north of the Gulf because of prevailing northerly winds. The roads were kept in good repair and were safe for the first time since the seventh century, when the conquests of Islam had severed communication between China and Europe.

This access lasted until 1370, when the Chinese attacked the Mongols, an event that heralded the decline of the Mongol Empire. The Chinese severed trade and contact with the Europeans and so terminated the land logistics systems across Asia.

Parallel to the Chinese successes in the Far East, the rise of the Ottomans led to endless battles with the outposts of Christendom, culminating in the fall of Constantinople in 1453. This meant that trade with China was not only severely curtailed at a time when the demand for exotic eastern products was rising, owing to the recovery of Europe from the plague and the stimulus of the Crusades, but also that Arab and Ottoman middlemen now controlled both land and sea routes to India and the Spice Islands via the Middle East. The Europeans who benefitted most from this set of circumstances were the Venetians and Genoese.

The importance of spices to the Europeans should not be underestimated. In the late Middle Ages, spices came from India, Ceylon, and the East Indies via Arab ships and were distributed throughout Europe by the Venetians. The spice routes were complicated; in the Far East,

Chinese sailors carried nutmeg and cloves in junks from the Spice Islands to Malacca; spices proceeded by sea from Malacca to India, this time carried in Arab, Malaysian, or Indian boats. The Indian coast of Malabar contained the spice ports that sold the Far Eastern products, cinnamon from Ceylon, and pepper from India. From this point the Arabs carried the spices to ports in Persia, Arabia, and East Africa. At the end of the fifteenth century, there were two alternate routes to the Mediterranean using two ports, Hormuz and Aden (Parry, 1967: 163-165). The route up the Red Sea required that the spices be transferred from the large *baghlas* to smaller coastal vessels for their ultimate destination in Alexandria. From Hormuz, *bouars* carried the spices up the Gulf into the Shatt al Arab, from whence they were transferred to caravans and sent overland either via Asia Minor to Constantinople or across Iraq via Baghdad to the Syrian port of Tripoli, the outlet for the great bazaar at Aleppo. At Alexandria and Tripoli, Venetian ships carried them to Venice and, hence, by land and sea to farther destinations in Europe.

The most popular spices were cloves, cinnamon, nutmeg, mace, and pepper. There were three uses for these spices: to flavor food and drink —and disguise the taste of rotten meat —to make perfume, and to use as medicine. During the late fourteenth and fifteenth centuries, demand for spices was so high that prices could quintuple at source over a five-year period.[1] Thus, since the European middle classes were prepared to pay large sums of money for spices, numerous entrepreneurial skills evolved to satisfy the market conditions and merchants, as a result, reaped high profits. As one nineteenth-century commentator wrote, the rare specimens of "elegancies" brought home by returning Crusaders created a desire of obtaining greater quantities of them among their countrymen and stimulated their dormant industry to cultivate, or manufacture, some commodity which they might give in exchange for the new objects of desire. Thus nations, hitherto sunk in listless indolence or only aroused from it, when hunger urged them to the chase or their chiefs led them to battle, acquired *INDUSTRY*, the only efficient and legitimate source of all other acquisitions and of national prosperity [Macpherson, 1812: 6].

Lack of maritime access thus spurred not only the Age of Discovery but a certain amount of intra-European production as well.

This, then, was the situation in the mid-fifteenth century: Europe was relatively prosperous because there was sufficient surplus wealth to spend on luxury goods from the east; trade with the east, however, was controlled by Arab and Turkish middlemen, and only the city states of Venice and Genoa were able to profit from the situation (Brown, 1902: 65). Attempts by the spice-consuming countries to break the Arab and Venetian stranglehold on the spice trade was a motivating factor of the Age of Discovery; and, although one should not overemphasize the present-day analogy with Middle East oil, the lessons are very pertinent. Impetus in the search for new routes also might have been provided by a tax newly imposed by the Ottomans on the Venetians and Genoese in 1460. The Ottomans extinguished the political dominion and privileged economic position of the Venetians and Genoese by abolishing their complete immunity from customs duties in that year. Duties were increased to five percent for non-Muslims (four percent for non-Ottoman Muslims) in that year, which surely further inflated European prices (Holt et al., 1970: 305).

To explain the upsurge of discovery from about the mid-fifteenth century through the next hundred years only on the grounds of economic incentives would be erroneous. Yet, there can be no doubt that the ultimate goal of economic rewards was never far from the minds of those who supported and undertook the search for new routes and new lands. The economic incentive that made the Portuguese so keen to find an Atlantic sea route to Asia was Arab, Venetian, and Genoese domination of the Mediterranean. Later, however, Spain and Britain had incentives to find alternative routes to break Portuguese control of the Cape routes; Magellan's famous voyage, for example, was an attempt to find a southwest route to the Indies for Spain.

The British were particularly interested in discovering new routes to the Indies and the sources of the spice trade. Being the northernmost European country of consequence, Britain had the highest spice prices. Attempts had been made to bypass the European middlemen by sending ships to the end of the caravan route. One enterprising gentleman who realized British merchants could make a fortune if they could find a short, northern route to the Indies was John Cabot. Although he was of Italian origin and had become a naturalized citizen of Venice, there is some evidence that shows he sought support from the Portuguese and Spanish to pioneer a short route to the Indies. However, it was in England that he was to receive the greatest backing when, in 1496, he was granted permission by Henry VII to sail across the Atlantic in search of a new route (Morison, 1978: 41).

The first country to exploit fully the new routes to the east was Portugal. Nevertheless, despite their efforts to establish the Cape route and open up the coast of Africa, the Portuguese dominated the spice trade only briefly. Although they had no problem securing spices, their parallel efforts to deny the trade to the Arabs led to endless skirmishes and taxed their limited resources. They were never able to conquer Aden, which would have given them control of the Red Sea route. Furthermore, rumors abounded in Europe that spices carried by Portuguese ships were of inferior quality to those obtained from the Arabs by the Venetians. This rumor may have been spread by the Venetians themselves, but there was also evidence that Portuguese ships suffered greatly during the rough passage from India. Therefore, it was probably true that some consignments of spices were soaked with salt water, which would certainly have affected their aroma. Another problem was that the Portuguese had little to offer the traders except bullion, while the Arabs carried many products considered desirable by the Indians and the Chinese.

The Dutch, not the Portuguese, eventually succeeded in cutting out the Arab traders from the spice markets by establishing a permanent presence in the Indian Ocean and dealing shrewdly with the local powers. The most effective long-term control over the sea routes and trade to the Indies, however, was eventually established by the British, who not only established a workable political relationship with the local rulers but were more successful at managing the finances of international trade than were their Dutch competitors.

This cursory review of the Age of Discovery has so far been presented almost entirely in economic and military terms. Yet, to appreciate fully the constellation of events that led to the great voyages of that era, it is necessary to appreciate the impact of ideology, the spirit of adventure, and the role of leadership that motivated the captains and visionaries of the time. Although greed cannot be discounted as a factor, additional incentives inspired the drama of those years. And this is the lesson for today: The United States will never reestablish its maritime superiority unless a similar combination of factors is put to work. The economic arguments may provide the political justification for greater exploitation of the seas, and the Soviet threat may provide the military justification; but unless and until the United States and its western allies regain a sense of confidence and ideology regarding their national policies, the contemporary crisis of inertia will continue.

The second lesson that has great relevance for today relates to the economic alternatives that can be adopted in times of constraint. With respect to spices, the Europeans faced a dilemma: their demand and the price of the supply. Although they were aware of the markup on spices, they nevertheless paid the price because the demand was present. Yet, it was price that provided the incentives to circumvent the Arabs and Venetian middlemen.

The similarities between the fifteenth-century spice trade and the contemporary oil trade can be overdrawn, but there are some common factors. Is oil more essential to twentieth-century industrial society than spices were to fifteenth-century society? If price is the criterion, then the answer may be no, since price markups in the spice trade were equally as dramatic as are present-day oil markups. But is not oil essential for production? Well, yes, but only in the short run, and the United States could manage with non-Arab oil if it really had to. The point is that the price of oil is still not high enough to persuade governments to enact emergency crash programs to ration and fund subsidies, though we may be approaching that point. As long as the supply is forthcoming, the price is still a secondary factor. But if interruptions in supply were to accelerate — assume, for instance, another Arab oil embargo, or a counterrevolution in Iran, or a Nigerian embargo — then not only would the price rise to meet the reduced supply but there would also almost certainly be greater incentives to avoid a similar situation in the future; that is, the incentives to seek alternatives would be absent. At this point, what would be required, if the fifteenth century is a guide, would be leadership, resolve, and a willingness to take risks and, if necessary, use force to prevent others exploiting our weaknesses.

MARITIME POWER: CONCEPTS AND COMPARISONS

Concepts

Maritime power, as a concept, requires careful definition in view of the varying interpretations of its meaning. Is maritime power an attribute that a state, or any other political unit, exercises over another? For example, by exploiting their maritime assets, do they influence the behavior of others? Or does the term refer to a set of conditions states have to meet in order to qualify being labeled a maritime power? To put it another way, can a state be a maritime power irrespective of its political, military, and economic relations with other states? Does the term power in the phrase a maritime power mean that a state uses the sea to exercise power over others or does power, in this context, refer to a more neutral condition in which the term is synonymous with state or nation? Thus, if we say country A is a maritime power, do we mean it uses its maritime attributes, whatever they are, to pursue its power relations with other states, or does it mean that country A is a maritime power because it makes use of its maritime attributes to survive and prosper irrespective of its overall status in the hierarchy of world power?

There are several important reasons for clarifying this point. First, there is genuine confusion concerning the

meaning of the term. Second, there is confusion in classifying those countries whose economic survival depends
on access to certain areas of the sea and those countries
which use the seas less for short-run economic survival
than for the projection of political and military power.

This confusion is further compounded if terms such as
sea power or naval power are introduced for, despite
some obvious similarities, there are important differences. Depending on one's definition of maritime power, a
great sea power need not be a great maritime power, even
though one usually follows from the other. A sea power
may be a state that has formidable naval strength — naval
in this case meaning ships and shipping capabilities that
permit the extensive use of military force for certain
missions. In contrast, a maritime power can be defined as
a state that makes extensive use of access to the sea and
sea resources to pursue economic activities with other
groups, which, in turn, influences its power relations with
them. These economic activities can include the transportation of land-based goods and services by sea or the
exploitation of sea-based resources.

By these definitions, there is no need for a major maritime power to develop a navy to protect its maritime
activity. In practice, however, all great maritime powers
have either developed naval forces to protect their maritime assets or have been eclipsed by adversaries who
either threaten their access to land-based resources and
trade or challenge their commercial activity at sea by
interfering with their rights of navigation. Similarly,
according to these definitions, a great sea power need not
be, in theory, a great maritime power, especially in the
present age of nuclear technology when deploying military forces to sea can be justified entirely outside the
maritime context, even though the evolution of most, but

not all, of the great sea powers has grown out of concern over the protection or extension of maritime activities.

Before proceding with a more formal classification of maritime powers and sea powers, it is appropriate to present a list of definitions of the terms used so far to explain why some will be used in this text and why others will not.

> *Maritime:* of or relating to navigation or commerce on and in the sea or on the seabed.
>
> *Naval:* of or relating to ships or shipping.
>
> *Maritime power:* no single definition is satisfactory, so three will be listed:
>
> (1) a state which makes extensive use of the seas and sea resources to sustain its economic growth;
>
> (2) a state which makes extensive use of the sea and sea resources for its economic growth, its political status, or its national security, or a combination of all three;
>
> (3) a state which makes extensive use of the seas and sea resources to sustain its economic growth and to project its political and military power to those overseas regions necessary for its economic well-being or national security.

Each of the three definitions of maritime power listed above poses different problems. The first definition is exclusive and narrow and to this extent is similar to the classical dictionary definition of maritime. It refers to extensive use of the sea and sea resources to sustain economic growth. However, it tells us nothing about power hierarchies, only about a specific dependency. Thus, by this definition, any state that makes extensive use of the seas is a maritime power, such as Iceland or Fiji. Indeed, if proportional uses of the sea for economic survival become the primary criterion for determining the maritime status of a country, Iceland would outrank the United States. It would seem, therefore, that this definition is inadequate if the concept of power is included in the term.

The second definition differs from the first in that it presumes to cover states that use the seas for more general goals than economic growth. Thus, this definition could cover a country with few economic interests in the maritime arena but used the seas for the projection of military power. In extremis, it could include a country that possessed only one or two nuclear-power and nuclear-armed submarines which, in theory, could project enormous military power from the sea in many regions of the world. The problem, then, with the second definition is that it is too inclusive and does not discriminate enough among a wide group of countries which, by its definition, could qualify for the title of maritime power.

Definition three reflects an attempt to bring more precision to the term without being too exclusive. It assumes that the economic exploitation of the seas is an essential element of being a maritime power but that it alone is insufficient. To qualify for the designation of power, a country must also use the seas to project its political and military power to those overseas regions where it has major economic and political interests. Thus, by this definition, a major maritime power would have to have the ability to protect its maritime interests against most political, economic, and military threats. This definition raises difficult questions concerning the status of countries like Japan, which, by most criteria, are formidable maritime powers except in their ability to project military force to secure their overseas maritime interests. The irony with Japan is that, while in most respects it is more truly a maritime power than the United States or the Soviet Union, as long as it remains dependent on the United States for the ultimate protection of its assets, it cannot be classified a major maritime power.

What emerges from the above discussion is that to qualify for the status of maritime power, a country must fulfill two conditions: significant dependency on access to the seas and significant ability to enforce its wishes if others challenge its maritime interests. Excluded from this category, therefore, are those countries which either meet none of the above conditions or only one of them. This suggests, in turn, that there is an important distinction between countries which, by this definition, are full-fledged maritime powers, those with the ability to project power overseas but with few maritime interests, those dependent on the seas and which aspire to be maritime powers, those which depend on the seas but can never realistically become maritime powers, and those that are neither dependent on the seas nor aspire to be maritime powers.

If these categories are now applied to the present countries of the world, what pattern emerges? Let it be assumed that each country fits into one of the following categories:

(1) maritime power;
(2) maritime capable, not maritime dependent;
(3) maritime dependent, aspiring maritime power;
(4) maritime dependent;
(5) landlocked and nonmaritime dependent.

If the presence of maritime power projection (categories 1 and 2) is termed sea power, and the absence of such capabilities is termed limited or no sea power (categories 3, 4, and 5), then the list can be refined as follows:

(1) maritime power (maritime dependent, significant sea power);
(2) sea power (significant sea power, little maritime dependency);

(3) maritime dependent—aspiring sea power;
(4) maritime dependent—not aspiring sea power;
(5) nonmaritime dependent—no sea power.

How would one proceed to classify the countries of the world based on these criteria? In simplistic terms, certain Western industrial powers fall into the first category of countries, while the Soviet Union falls into the second category. Thus, whereas Britain, France, West Germany, Japan, and the United States must have access to overseas resources and markets for their economic survival, the Soviet Union does not need similar access except as a bonus. Its primary interest in maritime activities relates to its political and military conflict with the Western industrial powers and China. An analysis of this classification suggests that there are considerable differences among the traditional maritime powers and that, in some ways, the United States and the Soviet Union have more common attributes than is often understood.

When analyzing the United States and Japan, nominally two maritime powers sharing a common political ideology (which, in turn, has resulted in similar economic systems and a shared concept of military security), we find they are very different in many ways. This is best illustrated by considering an extreme case: If all sea communication to both the United States and Japan from the rest of the world were severed, the United States would probably survive as an industrial democracy, whereas Japan would not. The United States, despite its massive overseas involvement and its growing overseas oil dependency, is and will remain a vast, well-endowed, continental power that has sufficient indigenous resources to sustain its current population at a tolerable level of welfare. Thus, although a policy of enforced continental self-sufficiency would cause very serious short-run dislocations in the economy, which, in turn, would have profound political effects, there is no reason why the United States could not survive as a strong industrial power, albeit with a very different set of limitations on economic growth and, therefore, material expectations. Given its geography, it would also be relatively immune from military attack other than by nuclear weapons. Japan, on the other hand, is much less capable of such long-term survival because of its lack of indigenous resources and large population. Furthermore, its close proximity to China and the Soviet Union would place its security in jeopardy in the event of aggressive ambitions by either of its neighbors.

To carry this argument a step further, we could distinguish between Japan—an insular, homogeneous, industrial state totally dependent on external sea lines of communication for all major natural resources—and the members of the European Economic Community (EEC)—a heterogeneous group of industrial and semiindustrial states adjacent to the Soviet Union, with considerable indigenous natural resources but not enough to maintain their current economic status. Thus, one means of classifying various states would be to rank-order them according to maritime dependency in peacetime and maritime dependency in wartime. The difference between the two orderings would reflect the degree to which dependency was a luxury or a necessity. The point is that a country like the United States or the Soviet Union could rank high in the peacetime column out of preference but low in the wartime column because of abundant indigenous natural resources. In reality, the distinction between peace and war is too arbitrary given the many nonwartime or crisis situations that can also put constraints on the freedom of the seas. But for the purpose of these hypothetical classifications of maritime powers, the distinction has validity.

Although there are similarities between the United States and the Soviet Union in that both are, in effect, continental powers, the differences are equally as important. The United States is generally classified a maritime power in part because of its early history as a maritime country, in part because of the massive increase in the size of its naval power and overseas deployment during and following World War II, partly because of its extensive and growing overseas trade, and also because its most important friends and allies are maritime powers or maritime-dependent powers.

The Soviet Union, on the other hand, does not have this history, nor is it or its allies presently as dependent on the seas (except for fish resources) as Western countries. Yet, the Soviet Union has a growing naval and merchant marine capability and is the world's second greatest sea power. This raises an interesting question. Does a great sea power eventually become a great maritime power by default or as a result of the deliberate pursuit of commercial maritime activities once it has become a sea power? To some extent, this depends on the definition given to the status "great sea power." In one sense, it could be argued that any country that deployed one nuclear-powered submarine armed with nuclear missiles would, in contemporary world terms, be a sea power by the most familiar yardstick of military strength—firepower. Yet, somehow this measurement does not seem to fit with common sense; for, by this criterion, Britain and France, with their small nuclear-powered ballistic missile submarine (SSBN) fleets, have greater comparative naval strength today vis-à-vis all states in the world except the United States and USSR than at any time in their history. The problem is that neither Britain or France can use its SSBN forces very effectively in the context of peacetime commercial and military power relations with other states. Only in the event of a major crisis or war would the SSBNs have a role, and even then it is assumed they would be of little use against low-level threats. To this extent, they are very different elements of sea power than the traditional gunboat.

The contrast between the gunboat as the symbol of a great power's willingness and ability to intervene to protect its interests and the SSBN is important. The appearance of a British gunboat in an Arabian port in the nineteenth century represented a different type of power than would be the case today if Britain deployed an SSBN into the Indian Ocean and announced it had targeted an Arab country with nuclear weapons. In fact, it is incredible to think of that event taking place except in the most dire circumstances.

It therefore may be more sensible to refer to a major sea power as a country that uses the sea on a continuing basis to exercise power relations with other states. It follows that those countries capable of challenging others for the use of the seas can be regarded as threats to the major sea powers; and within the hierarchy of sea powers, the country able to downgrade or limit the capacity of others to use the seas for what they regard as their vital interests can be regarded as having superiority. According to this definition, the concept of superiority refers less to the comparative size or configuration of competing maritime forces than to the ability of one side to deny the other uses of the seas, an ability which need not be achieved solely with naval forces. Furthermore, the country with the greatest dependency on the seas will have the most to lose in the event of a confrontation. More specifically, the Soviet Union, because it is less dependent on the seas, is able to challenge and perhaps even exercise maritime superiority over the United States, even though its naval forces are presently inferior to those of the Western alliance.

Comparisons:
The Legacy of Alfred Mahan[2]

In view of the importance attached to the theories of Alfred Mahan, it is useful to review what he said about maritime power, what was missing from his writings, and what his legacy really is. We will discuss his elements of sea power by comparing the United States and the Soviet Union. We will illustrate the weakness of his arguments by showing how the decline of his example, Britain, had a great deal to do with technical change and logistics infrastructure, two elements he tended to downplay in his formal writings. Finally, we will review his legacy in the context of present U.S. defense policy.

Mahan's Elements of Seapower

In his basic work, *The Influence of Seapower Upon History*, Mahan lists six basic elements that determine the sea power of nations: geographical position; physical conformation, including climate and natural production; extent of territory; size of population; character of the people; and character of government and national institutions. Many of the examples he draws upon to justify this list make good sense even today. Before discussing what is missing from the list, let us consider the classical elements and relate them to the contemporary environment.

Geographical position, physical conformation, and extent of territory. Mahan's first three elements of sea power overlap considerably and can best be treated as one single category in view of the geographic component of each element. Despite the advent of the intercontinental missile, geographical position remains a critical factor in determining the relative strength and vulnerability of states. For all conceivable military conflicts short of general nuclear war, geography plays a role in influencing strategic posture. Even in the event of general nuclear war, geography would not necessarily be irrelevant but would depend on the nature of the nuclear exchange and the relative balance of power between adversaries after the initial nuclear exchange. The concept of broken-backed warfare, coined by Churchill in the early 1950s, referred to an ongoing war fought by conventional means following crippling nuclear attacks, metaphorically, broke the backs of the competing states. In this situation, geographical access to and control of the sea would play a vital role in determining the survival capabilities of the major adversaries.

In all other probable military scenarios, the role of geography will continue to be a key element in the military balance. In more specific terms, any comparison of U.S.-Soviet maritime power must pay special attention to the major geographic asymmetries that influence each country. The United States is geographically vulnerable in several different ways. First, its outer territories — Alaska, the Aleutians, and the Hawaiian archipelago — are located in areas far from the continental United States and, in the case of Alaska and the Aleutians, in close proximity to the Soviet Union. Second, many of the United States' most important allies and trading partners are located far across the oceans; therefore, there is the need for a forward deployment strategy, which has economic, military, and political liabilities. Third, the United States, being a maritime power, has most of its population located within 200 miles of the seaboard, which has serious implications in the event of an attack by Soviet submarines against the U.S. urban and industrial complex.

To offset these vulnerabilities, however, the United States is endowed with several important geographical advantages. First, because it is a continental power separated from Europe, Asia, and Africa by two oceans, it is relatively immune from threats from adjacent countries and will remain so for the foreseeable future. Although there have been periods in U.S. history when foreign powers, in cooperation with Mexico or Canada, have posed a threat, these periods seem unlikely for the next decade unless there are serious crises developing in relations with Mexico or Canada. Second, and related to Mahan's second element (physical conformation), the United States has excellent harbors spread along its three coasts. These provide open access to the high seas and, with the exception of the Caribbean ports, are located far from possible enemy positions. Third, the United States has a large continental territory and has access to several important distant strategic islands, including Hawaii.

In comparison, the Soviet Union faces a different set of geographical problems. It is a vast, underdeveloped, continental land power with an extreme climate that has had a profound influence on its history and on the psychological attitudes of its people toward the development of the interior and the search for maritime access. The size and climate of the Soviet Union have offset the disadvantages of sharing borders with Europe, the Middle East, and the Far East. Neither Napoleon nor Hitler were able to overcome the Russian winter, and the Soviet population today is still much farther inland and removed from direct threats than is the case with the United States. However, the very size and climate of the Soviet Union are also military disadvantages. Vital land lines of communication between European Russia—the industrial heartland—and its Far Eastern reaches remain vulnerable; and although the construction of the new BAM railroad will help alleviate the dependency on the Trans-Siberian railroad, the Soviet Union is, by U.S. standards, still backward in terms of transportation and still relies heavily on waterborne transportation for much of its commercial activity.

The Soviet Union's most serious vulnerablility in this category is the restraints on its access to the high seas. Although the USSR has less need of such access than the maritime powers, there has long been a historical interest in securing access to the warmwater ports of the Indian Ocean and Mediterranean Sea. Moreover, since those days Soviet economic interests in the seas have increased, especially in fishing and offshore mining.

In military terms, the Soviet's access problem can be broken down by naval district. Each of the four Soviet fleets—Northern, Baltic, Black Sea, and Pacific—faces dangers as a result of the unique configuration of the Soviet Union. The Baltic and Black Sea fleets are hemmed in by the Danish and Turkish Straits, while the Northern and Pacific fleets face the prospect of egress to the high seas through sea areas close to U.S. and Allied naval and air forces. The fleets must also traverse narrow waterways, especially in winter in the case of the Northern fleet. Although the Soviet Union has greatly improved its capability for fighting its way into the areas containing the approaches to the four naval districts, its capacity to project power beyond the immediate area of its geographical landmass could be curtailed, especially if the Western naval powers were agreeable to offensive action against targets such as the Kola bases.

Soviet vulnerability in the Kola Peninsula is one of the most striking examples of this type of geographical asymmetry between the two superpowers. Kola has become the most important maritime base for the Soviet Union because from this area it deploys the bulk of its

SSBN force and from here large numbers of the Soviet fishing activities in the North Atlantic are launched. Kola is adjacent to NATO territory in north Norway and its inland harbors are vulnerable to Allied mining operation. It is from Kola, too, that Soviet naval aviation (SNA) can deploy into the North Atlantic and pose threats to the Allied sea lines of communication necessary to maintain the viability of the NATO Alliance in the event of a major war with the Warsaw Pact countries.

In physical conformation and extent of territory, the United States and the Soviet Union have advantages over most other powers in the world. Both are well-endowed with natural resources and could probably survive on their own resources if they had to. Despite growing U.S. dependency on foreign resources, especially oil, this extra demand is that of a peacetime free market. In the event of crises, the United States has enough oil to keep its industry and military forces operational and enough surplus to provide oil to allies for military operations. Similarly, the Soviet Union has an abundance of resources and will be able to feed its population at a level of nutrition necessary for survival despite the all-too-apparent weaknesses of Soviet agriculture.

Size of population, character of people, and character of government. The second category of elements Mahan discusses are the human, as distinct from geographical and physical, elements. In many ways his observations about these factors seem more simplistic today than his geographical observations.

Since Mahan's day, the level of analysis of human factors as a component of international power relations has become much more sophisticated and empirical. Mahan paid particular attention to the number of people who were trained in maritime skills — a large seafaring population was clearly an advantage. While this factor is still important, modern technology has obviated much of the need for seafaring traditions. Some of the most important sailors on a modern ship are the computers that plot and direct the ship's complicated systems; and although the importance of skilled maritime traditions should not be undervalued, the sophisticated activities that take place on board a modern ship in most circumstances short of war require skills different from those referred to by Mahan. Furthermore, many modern skills can be learned by nonseafaring persons, although, from the point of view of morale, a preference for the nautical life is probably an asset.

Undoubtedly, maritime skills remain an important element of any country's power if it wishes to exploit its maritime environment; but the question is whether these skills can be regarded today as unique—that is, nontransferable with other national skills— or whether or not they can be substituted to a greater degree than was possible in the past. Put more bluntly, life on board a modern oil tanker, container ship, or even warship bears little resemblance to operations in large vessels in World War II, let alone at the turn of the century. Modern ships can operate in virtually any sea conditions. Major repairs of equipment are usually undertaken on board; and navigation, while occasionally a problem, has nothing like the uncertainty that bedeviled the most routine voyages in Mahan's day.

All this is not to say that seamanship has no place in modern maritime forces; rather, fewer members of the crew need to be skilled in the arts, as distinct from the sciences, of their new profession. In theory, this means that a country with very little maritime tradition could be capable of operating a modern maritime force in a much shorter time than was the norm in the past. This is not the same as being able to operate effectively a navy in combat conditions, but it does mean that routine commercial operations at sea can now be practiced by increasing numbers of countries if they so wish.

Mahan's Missing Elements: The Dynamics of Technology and Logistics

Perhaps because he was living and writing at the peak of Britain's worldwide maritime supremacy and, as an American, he was seeking ways to ensure that the United States learned the right lessons from the British experience, it is not surprising that Mahan's writings on the elements of sea power pay insufficient attention to the role technology and logistics had come to play in enabling Britain to remain the world's maritime superpower — and how these same factors led to Britain's naval decline.

To understand the role of technology and logistics upon maritime power at the end of the nineteenth century, it is necessary to go back to the 1830's, when the invention of the steam engine heralded the beginning of a revolution in land transportation with the development of the railway. The railway was such an obvious improvement over coach and horse that soon it was widely accepted. There were greater problems with the application of the steam engine for maritime use, however. The first steam engines were used to supplement sail power and were installed to drive large, unwieldy paddles. While paddle steamers made sense for certain waterways, such as the large rivers of the United States, they were not reliable for heavy sea conditions and could not replace sail on most ocean voyages. Furthermore, steam engines burned coal or wood, and both fuels were unavailable on the high seas unless the ship was accompanied by a support vessel. Along river and railroads, however, steam engines could easily be refueled by stockpiling coal and wood at intervals along the route.

The first breakthrough in maritime steam engine technology came with the invention of the screw propeller, which made steam-engined vessels more stable and capable of higher, more sustained speeds. Gradually, the screw propeller replaced the sail as the predominant form of propulsion aboard contemporary warships, although until the late 1880s sail was still used on most classes of vessels. With the gradual acceptance of the steam engine, dependency on coal increased, although it was not possible to use ordinary coal for most maritime operations, especially if the ships operated in tropical climates. The preferred coal was one that was relatively smokeless and easy to handle in hot climates; it would not disintegrate. A near monopoly on this type of coal was held by Britain.

Throughout the latter half of the nineteenth century, Britain was the king of coal; in fact, the British empire was not only the world's largest coal producer but also the largest exporter. In contemporary terms, Britain was the Saudi Arabia of coal. Coal not only came from Britain itself but from India, South Africa, and Canada. The Royal Navy set up an elaborate network of coaling stations across the globe, especially along the main trade routes of the empire, and kept its ships supplied with British-controlled coal. No other country was capable of establishing such a worldwide network and no other country tried; although Japan had control of a few coaling stations in the Far East, and the United States had coaling stations in the Caribbean and Pacific. The other great European powers, especially Germany and Russia, were very dependent on access to foreign coal when they wanted to deploy their fleets far from their own lands.

There could be no better example of this dependency than the problems faced by the Russian Grand Fleet in 1904—1905 when it made its fateful voyage to the Far East from the Baltic to join other Russian forces in the war against Japan. By the time the fleet of 45 ships arrived at Tsushima Strait in 1905, wear and tear on the ships had been disastrous. Although Admiral Togo deserves credit for the brilliance of his campaign against the Grand Fleet, Russia's lack of preparedness undoubtedly played an important role in the overwhelming Japanese victory. One reason for Russia's defeat was that Britain had made it difficult for the Russians to obtain coal en route. In fact, because of its alliance with Japan, Britain had denied coal to the Russian fleet, although it was sold to German civilian ships, which subsequently rendezvoused with the Russians to supply them. The point here is that the logistics of operating a large coal-burning fleet were horrendous. Coal, bulky and messy, could be moved around the ship only by use of shovels; thus, large numbers of the crew were permanently involved in coaling operations—a very inefficient use of manpower.

Partly because of its great self-sufficiency in maritime operations, Britain was able to fight the very unpopular Boer War in 1898-1903 without having to worry about direct foreign intervention. This is not to say that Britain feared no attacks against the Empire, but that in the specific theater of South Africa, British power was unchallenged primarily because of its maritime superiority and control of the logistics of supply. To this extent there is a similarity with the U.S. position during the Vietnam war. Although the U.S. intervention was extremely unpopular, no foreign power—not even the Soviet Union—was capable of preventing U.S. intervention by counterintervention or interposition. How far the Boer War—which, incidentally, heralded the end of Britain's world supremacy—parallels the U.S. decline after Vietnam is an interesting question. There are certainly analogies, perhaps the most ominous of which is that, by the time Britain next had to fight a major war, it had lost its maritime self-sufficiency. For technical and military reasons Churchill and the Admiralty decided in 1911 to change the engines in Royal Navy ships from coal- to oil-burners. The strategic implications of this move were far-reaching and were not anticipated by Mahan.

The Shift from Coal to Oil

Military arguments for and against the shift to oil propulsion could be neatly separated into the tactical and logistical. From almost every operational perspective, oil was a godsend; it was easier to handle and required less crew to operate. This meant great savings in manpower. Oil could be stored in more obscure parts of the ship, thereby leaving more room for ammunition. Underway and port replenishment were simpler and less time-consuming. Most important, oil-fired engines performed better and at greater sustained speeds than did coal engines. A difference of five knots at full steam could make all the difference, and the anticipated higher speeds of the new German dreadnoughts convinced the Admiralty that, weight for weight, the change to oil would bring great tactical benefit. Other benefits of oil included the fact that oil-fueled engines could operate on crude oil purchased from virtually any storage facility in the world.

Offsetting these advantages, however, was the realization that Britain had neither oil of its own nor ready access to oil. The world's leading oil producers at the time were the United States, Russia, and Mexico. It was not in Britain's interests to rely on these countries for the strategic defense of the Empire. Yet, as the arms race with Germany accelerated, the tactical advantages of oil seemed overwhelming.

Thus, Churchill made the decision to abandon unilaterally the benefits of coal self-sufficiency. To compensate, however, the Foreign Office was instructed to press for special claims on the newly discovered oil resources of

Persia and Mesopotamia. Although Britain had always had major strategic stakes in the Gulf region because of the proximity of its arch-rival Russia, oil now became another reason for increasing British interests in the region. In fact, by the outbreak of war in 1914, both Britain and Russia were seriously concerned about their respective oil supplies from the Gulf and from Baku in view of the threat to these areas posed by the Turkish Army.

World War I demonstrated the importance of secure oil lines of communication. The British campaign in the Middle East, which culminated in Allenby's defeat of the Turkish forces in Palestine, was, in part, motivated by the need to protect the route to India and Gulf oil. Not that this was enough. British and French dependency on the United States for oil proved to be one of the most important logistics crises of the war. At one point, Britain was on the verge of ending hostilities because of the effectiveness of the German U-boat campaign against the oil sea lines of communication (SLOCs) across the Atlantic, and it was only the belated use of the convoy system that overcame the U-boat threat.

The purpose of this footnote to history is to show how strategic dependencies can change very quickly as a result of technical change and the geographic location of resources. From being the coal king in 1900, Britain rapidly moved to the position of an oil-dependent nation, which, in turn, led to a changed British perspective on areas such as the Persian Gulf. Furthermore, this shift in Britain's power was taken deliberately for short-term tactical reasons and was not the result of incompetence or bad luck.

In contemporary maritime policy, as long as a country has superiority in its fighting ships and the worldwide logistical infrastructure necessary to support them in battle, the benefits can be great. If logistical self-sufficiency is not possible or is eroded, however, the ability to project maritime power to remote areas may be impossible. This constraint, not inadequacies in weapons systems or ship performance, may be the most significant limiting factor. Today, both the United States and the Soviet Union face limitations on their respective abilities to operate their blue-water navies when and where they like. For, although both countries possess global navies, both—but especially the USSR—have an inadequate world-wide infrastructure to support much more than presence missions or one-shot encounters. In this regard, the United States is still better-endowed to conduct contained, high-tempo operations in areas such as the South China Sea and even the Indian Ocean. But as long as the Soviet Union has no major base along the Indian Ocean littoral, it cannot contemplate large-scale military operations with its navy in Africa and the Middle East. If, however, the Soviet Union were to gain such access, this alone would have a major impact on the naval balance of power in the region. In this regard, it should be stressed that any Soviet military presence in Iran would give it access to the warm water ports of Bandar Abbas, which would have direct land communication with the Soviet Union proper. Thus, in this case, a shift in the land balance could have a decisive effect upon the maritime balance, drawing attention once more to the importance of the linkage between these two elements in the power equation between nations.

The most important legacy of Alfred Mahan is not to be found in his technical writings or even in his classic work *The Influence of Seapower Upon History*. His great relevance today is his political vision, his sense of destiny, and his efforts to persuade his own government that its future greatness lay in the further exploration of its maritime assets. His message for today would be that unless the United States has a greater sense of purpose and seeks practical ways to fulfill it, it will surely decline as a world power.

What does this mean for the United States? First, the United States has abundant maritime assets that it can and should exploit, ranging from further development and control of its own immensely rich offshore maritime resources to greater investments in maritime technology for both military and nonmilitary purposes. Second, in a sense most applicable to Mahan's basic message, the United States must make a greater effort to extend and exploit its lead in air and space technology, for it is in this medium—especially in outer space—that important determinants of international power will be decided in the twenty-first century. In fact, it would be appropriate to modify the catchwords of earlier geopolitical strategists, such as Sir Halford Mackinder and Giulio Douhet, and propose the dictum that in the future the country that controls outer space will control the maritime environment, and the country that controls the maritime environment will control the world. The third message derives from the second: The United States must rediscover the political will necessary for new progress to be made.

THE EMERGING
MARITIME ENVIRONMENT

In recent years, a number of factors have changed the nature of the maritime environment and have begun to pose challenges to the preeminent maritime role the United States has held since the end of World War II. These factors include (1) The growing dependency of the Western industrial world and many emerging countries in the Third World on the seas for the transit of raw materials, the export of products, and the supply of energy, minerals, and food; (2) a new Law of the Sea, which, paralleling increased demands for uses of the oceans, promises to alter radically the traditional freedom of access enjoyed by the major maritime powers in the past; (3) the formidable growth of Soviet military power and the Soviet Union's willingness to use its navy to project power far from its shores; and (4) the growth of sea-denial capabilities by a number of less industrial states that have many unresolved conflicts with the maritime powers and with their own neighbors over territorial demarcations and access rights.

It is the purpose here to discuss the military impact of some of these trends on U.S. maritime policy — in particular, on military access rights and the likelihood that maritime commerce along SLOCs will be more vulnerable to military attack.

Until the 1960s, the majority of countries of the world subscribed to a three-mile limit for national sovereignty over adjacent waters. However, as a result of the 1958 continental shelf agreement, which decreed that states had the sole right to exploit the resources of their continental shelves out to the 200-meter point or median line, it became increasingly clear that, as more and more valuable resources were economically retrievable from the seabed, it would be necessary to refine further the laws of access to these resources. In addition, the worldwide growth of fishing was beginning to pose problems of jurisdiction and conservation. During the 1950s, the protein-hungry nations of Eastern Europe, the Soviet Union, Japan, and the Koreas expanded their fishing industries, and some — especially the Russians and the Japanese — began to fish in distant waters using new, highly efficient techniques, including factory ships, sonar, and radar.

Furthermore, economic pressures combined with new technologies made the sea more competitive at the same time that decolonization was taking place and the countries of the Third World were beginning to challenge the traditional concepts of international law, including the Law of the Sea, which they argued, had been set up for the convenience of the traditional maritime powers and was therefore another legacy of colonial exploitation.

The most important issues at stake in the new Law of the Sea were the extent of sovereignty, the economic rights of littoral states over the continental shelf beyond the territorial sea (the exclusive economic zone—EEZ) and the ownership and rights regarding minerals and other products found in the high seas, (that is, the remaining areas of the oceans not covered by the former sets of claims).

Some consensus on these issues seems to be emerging, including principles that will extend territorial seas out to 12 miles, establish exclusive economic zones out to 200 miles (inclusive of the territorial sea) or to median lines, and establish an international regime to manage the exploitation of the high seas.

In strategic terms, the first two issues give rise to questions of most importance to the maritime powers, especially the extension of territorial seas from 3 to 12 miles, which will affect over 100 straits. Strategic passageways such as Gibraltar, Malacca, Hormuz, Bab el Mandeb, and Dover will fall under the jurisdiciton of the littoral states. Although the negotiators at the Law of the Sea conference have gone to great lengths to ensure that traditional access through these straits will be maintained, some believe that the new laws, together with the natural increase in maritime traffic, will inevitably lead to greater restrictions on access. The traffic problems in some of the most crowded straits (for example, Malacca and Dover) have already given rise to strict rules of the road, which, if not enforced, could lead to serious accidents. The ecological effects of tanker mishaps have confirmed fears over safety at sea, and if we add the potential for nuclear-powered ships colliding with supertankers or running aground in narrow shallows, it does not take much imagination to see how, in times of poor political relations between countries, littoral states may enforce strict access rules through waterways that will be nominally justified on the grounds of safety and pollution.[3]

The point is not that the great powers in a crisis situation will be prevented from using strategic straits — although this could happen — but that the political costs to be paid for defying the littoral state will undoubtedly be higher. Furthermore, if it is assumed that overflight rights could be equally affected by the extension of jurisdiction out to 12 miles, this might have an equally significant impact on great power crisis diplomacy. Since one of the great attributes of air power is speed, any factor that works to delay flight time, such as rerouting or the need to ask permission to overfly, would naturally downgrade the value of this capability. As Ambassador Elliot Richardson said in a recent speech, "True, once a catastrophic crisis is upon us, the question of risk and cost may be cast aside. It is in our preventive missions and in our capacity to deter such a crisis that restraints are most acutely felt."

The establishment of zones may have a similar strategic impact on the major maritime powers. Although the littoral states will have no legal jurisdiction over movement through the zones, there may come a time when, dependent on the level of economic activity and size of the zone, greater monitoring will be necessary.

Although this creeping jurisdiction is not inevitable, especially if the United States or other maritime powers make a conscious effort in Law of the Sea discussions to improve their access rights, it seems likely that before the end of the century the U.S. Navy will have to test its rights of access through certain zones. For unless these trends are forcefully challenged, new perceptions of territory or, more properly, territoriality, could lead to the de facto jurisdiction of littoral states over huge new areas of the oceans.

Increased use of the seas as a source of minerals, energy, and animal protein is itself a result of two phenomena—increasing demand for these products, especially from the industrial countries, and improved technology that has opened up hitherto impenetrable areas. Perhaps the most dramatic examples have been in the development of major offshore oil and gas facilities in areas such as the Arctic Sea and the North Sea and in the increased use of extremely efficient techniques for harvesting fish including factory ships equipped with long-term refrigeration facilities.

In some respects this new maritime technology is in its infancy. For instance, the Prudhoe Bay oil fields have required the use of special techniques for cold-weather drilling and operations that have great implications for further oil development throughout the Arctic basin, including the Soviet arctic. Also, the Prudhoe Bay complex required the construction of the world's longest, most expensive oil pipeline from the north slope to the terminal facilities at Valdez in Southern Alaska. Given the vast amount of oil that, in all probability, remains untapped in the Arctic region and the experience gained at Prudhoe Bay, by the turn of the century some of the Canadian and Soviet fields will probably become operational, which will contribute to the expansion of the overall logistical infrastructure of the Arctic. Similarly, the experiences with the North Sea oil development are likely to be applied to further oil developments in the Norwegian Sea north of the sixty-second parallel and in the Atlantic Ocean to the west of the Shetland Islands.

The overall impact of these northern oil developments will be to heighten the pace of economic activity in the region and generally increase the political sensitivity of these formerly remote maritime regions. This, in turn, will inevitably lead to greater efforts by the littoral states to monitor and police offshore and onshore activities. This situation can lead to greater cooperation between adjacent states but also contains the ingredients for conflict if other issues such as fishing rights and military security become involved. Thus, although there may be increased Norwegian-Soviet cooperation in the distribution of Arctic oil, the same countries also run the risk of antagonizing each other in view of the strategic importance of the Kola peninsula to the Soviet Union and of the North Cape of Norway to the NATO powers.

As the remote areas achieve greater economic and strategic importance, littoral states will change their political perceptions about their own territoriality. This, together with the new legal regimes, may well result in the extension of the concept of national sovereignty to cover the new area. Athough this may not be codified — at least beyond the 12-mile limit — there may be a major increase in areas of direct littoral responsibility, which will undoubtedly result in greater political and bureaucratic initiatives to establish laws and regulations to achieve security for the activities in the area.

Growth of the Soviet Navy

The emergence of the Soviet navy as a global force poses different problems for different regions of the world. Although students of Soviet naval affairs and the U.S.-Soviet naval balance continue to debate whether the primary purpose of Soviet naval expansion is still basically defensive or whether it has assumed a more aggressive offensive posture, for most countries of the world Soviet naval strength has to be seen in potentially offensive terms. This is particularly true for the littoral states located near the four major egress points for the Soviet fleet: the Kola peninsula, the Baltic, the Black Sea and eastern Mediterranean, and the Soviet Far East. Thus, the buildup of the Soviet northern fleet at Murmansk must be seen as a potential power projection by Norway, and to a lesser extent by the United Kingdom. Similarly, the expansion of the Soviet and Warsaw Pact naval forces in the Baltic has had an immediate impact on the perceptions of Sweden, Norway, Denmark, and West Germany. The Black Sea fleet and the permanent establishment of a Soviet Mediterranean squadron represent a significant shift in the balance of power in the region, with important military significance for Turkey, Greece, Cyprus, Egypt, Israel, Lebanon, and Syria. In the east, Japan, China, and the Koreas are directly affected by the Soviet naval buildup at Vladivostok.

No matter what Soviet plans are for the use of its maritime forces in the event of global war with the United States and its allies, in the context of peacetime and regional crises the new navy gives the Soviet leadership an added instrument of political-military power that can only help the overall capabilities of the Soviet Union to influence regional power politics in its favor.

This is not to say that the balance of naval power in the area has decisively shifted in favor of the Soviet Union, for such calculations or estimates can be made only if one assesses the entire spectrum of political and military tasks for which naval forces are used. It is probably still the case that in areas such as the eastern Mediterranean and the Far East, Western naval forces retain considerable advantages in regional crises and nonnuclear conflicts involving both sides. The residual Western superiority, however, has less relevance for peacetime presence missions or in the context of Soviet—and Soviet surrogate—local power confrontations not directly involving the United States.

Consider, for instance, the status of USSR-Japanese maritime relations. Japan's bilateral relations with the

Soviet Union involve several unresolved maritime problems, including the demarcation of fishing rights and the Soviet occupation of Sakhalin and the north of Hokkaido island. There have been numerous incidents— some of them violent—between the two countries in the past decade over illegal fishing activity, and recently there has been increasing harassment of Japanese fishing vessels by Soviet ships and aircraft. This, in addition to the Soviet reinforcement sent to garrisons on the island of Sakhalin, lends credence to the belief that the Soviet Union is using its formidable maritime power in the region to intimidate Japan and signal its determination to strengthen its political, economic, and military base in the region.

What this means is that the growth of Soviet regional naval power is bound to put greater constraints on the deployment and access of Western maritime forces in areas such as the Sea of Japan, the East and South China Seas, the Indian Ocean, the Mediterranean, and the Barents Sea, especially in peacetime or crisis situations when the incentives to avoid confrontation with the Soviet navy may balance the desire to show the flag.

Impact of Smaller Maritime Forces

The growth of small maritime forces over the coming decades can be expected to continue, especially in those regions where local conflicts over offshore resources remain unresolved. Although this diffusion of maritime forces is part of the more general growth of military power in the less developed countries, there are special reasons why it has occurred and why it will continue. Some of the reasons relate directly to the need to police newly acquired territorial seas and exclusive economic zones and to establish a maritime constabulary force to protect resources, deny access to interlopers, and, in some areas, deter increasing incidents of piracy and smuggling. Other reasons relate to more traditional concerns about political-military relations with neighbors with whom outstanding conflicts still exist.

In order to exercise surveillance over large sea areas, which is a prerequisite to any form of control, it is necessary for a littoral state to have at its disposal reconnaissance systems capable of operating in most weather conditions to distances of 200 miles or more. Depending on geography and the prevailing climate, these tasks vary greatly in terms of difficulty. Most less developed countries are simply not able to survey in any constant and systematic manner the vast area of water over which they have, or soon will have, rights and jurisdiction. Furthermore, if a reconnaissance system is able to give positive identification to unknown vessels, civilian or military, it usually requires close visual contact. Thus, the identification of specific fishing vessels is often not possible with high-flying aircraft, let alone satellites (assuming they are available); the constabulary force must rely, instead, on low-flying aircraft or sea-surface patrol craft.

In order to demonstrate the difficulty of positive offshore surveillance, the British example with the North Sea operations is illuminating and shows why less developed countries will need to improve greatly their capabilities if they are to exercise minimum control over their sea areas. In the British case the problem began with the de facto extension of British jurisdiction in the North Sea and Atlantic to the median line with adjacent countries, or to 200 miles. Within this new British territory many economic and military activities take place, including normal seaborne and airborne traffic, offshore oil drilling production and supply, multinational fishing operations, and substantial NATO and Warsaw Pact military activity. Thus, in a single day, there are literally hundreds of ships and aircraft crisscrossing the British sector of the North Sea and North Atlantic including hundreds of helicopter flights a week to North Sea oil rigs. In the case of fishing vessels, very strict rules are set by the British government regarding the number, type, and time frame of foreign vessels that can fish—and the fish they can catch. The policing of the fishing areas, therefore, requires that each vessel be identified and, if necessary, inspected. Herein lies the problem. If Britain simply banned all foreign fishing vessels, it would be a matter of identifying foreign vessels and taking immediate action against the interlopers. Such an outright ban would be unacceptable, however, because of Britain's broader economic and political relations with its neighbors.

The practical tasks involved in identifying specific fishing vessels are formidable. The most common method is to fly so-called tapestry missions with Nimrod aircraft over a given sector of the North Sea. (The British sector of the North Sea is divided into three operational zones: one Nimrod can cover about half of one zone in a ten-hour flight if weather conditions are good.) In order to identify the vessel and also to check on oil rigs, the Nimrod has to fly for about ten hours with a full crew at between 200 and 500 feet, between 200 and 300 knots, and take photographs of the registration numbers on each fishing vessel. This in possible only if the identification marks on the fishing vessel are clear enough to be photographed and if the weather conditions permit good visibility. Once the vessel has been photographed, it may take several hours before a positive identification can be made, although this process can eventually be speeded up. It can take even longer before a surface vessel can intercept a suspected violator, by which time, of course, the vessel may have slipped back across a zone or into the high seas.

Admittedly, the North Sea is very busy and the British are trying to enact complicated laws, but it should also be borne in mind that over the past few years Britain has had several serious fishing disputes with friendly governments such as Holland and West Germany, which further points up the potential for problems when economic pressures exist in a complicated legal environment. How much more likely, then, that in those regions of the less developed world where the close relations of Britain and Holland do not exist, similar problems will pose much greater difficulties. The most likely arenas for this kind of competition are the South and East China Seas.

Another, and in some ways equally interesting, example is the situation in the Southeast Pacific and relations between the tiny new island republics as they grapple with the problems of independence. For thousands of years, island groups such as Fiji lived in harmony with their neighbors, who were located hundreds of miles away across open sea. With the establishment of extended sovereignty and economic zones, boundaries of these groups of islands have become contiguous. Overnight, Fijians have found that their distant neighbors are, literally, their next-door neighbors. With this has come a concern about policing fishing zones which are believed to contain extremely valuable resources. Thus, Fiji is developing a navy primarily to protect its exclusive economic zone, yet its ability to police effectively the claims under its jurisdiction is small, if it exists at all.

The technical requirements for successful constabulary forces are formidable and involve a combination of land-based systems, especially radar; land-based maritime reconnaissance and, possibly, strike aircraft; and surface vessels capable of long distances and equipped for search and intercept missions. Over the next 20 years or so, the demand for these systems is bound to increase; with it will come the beginnings of a basic infrastructure from which small constabulary forces can expand into small maritime forces.

Irrespective of policing duties, increasing numbers of the less developed countries perceive a requirement for larger maritime forces in view of military rivalry with their neighbors. Most of these rivalries are long-standing and existed before the current spate of conflicts over offshore resources. The best evidence of this trend is to be found in the statistics of arms transfers to these countries for maritime missions. The data show that the transfer of patrol boats, maritime patrol aircraft, ship-to-shore cruise missiles, inshore submarines, and smaller destroyer-type vessels is growing and is part of the overall trend of an increased military build-up in the less developed world.

The quality and size of maritime forces of the less developed countries vary greatly from region to region. Some countries, such as India, boast a relatively large naval inventory that, in microcosm, reflects the similar equipment and organization of the Western and Soviet navies, including an aircraft carrier with a complement of strike aircraft. Other navies—Israel's, for instance—are smaller but emphasize missile and fast patrol boats and have as their primary purpose control of the sea in the event of war. The navies of South America have more traditional missions akin to those of India, while the navies of southern African countries, with the exception of Nigeria, are primarily designed for coastal patrol.

What does this mean for Western access? It has been suggested, for instance, that several less developed countries are developing what can only be described as a sea-denial capability which, under certain specific circumstances, might place military constraints on the navies of the industrial countries. Here it should be noted that sea-denial capabilities can involve the use of land forces as well as maritime forces, depending on the particular sea area which is to be contested. Generally, narrow straits can be controlled with a land force, while martime forces are necessary for sea denial offshore. A review of the spread of sea-denial systems to less developed countries reveals that a sizable number of these countries have, or will have, in their inventories conventional submarines, missile patrol boats, and maritime reconnaissance and strike aircraft. Many countries have mine-laying capabilities, although mine-sweeping is not high on their list of priorities.

Thus, increasing numbers of less developed countries are able to exercise sea denial in increasing numbers of sea areas. But the important question is what this means for the maritime powers of the West and, for that matter, the Soviet Union, all of whom have placed great reliance on traditional concepts of freedom of the seas. Can the less developed countries currently deny the maritime powers and the Soviet Union passage through critical waterways? Will they be able to do so in the future?

The answer to these questions depends on the particular circumstances of an encounter. In a peacetime environment where none of the industrial powers is likely to be prepared to use force, the military ability of littoral states to deny passage is likely to be high. However, if such confrontations developed into a more serious crisis, there might come a point when the maritime powers would be prepared to use force to secure access to these waterways. In this case, the outcome of the confrontation would become dependent on the military calculations. Against some of the more powerful less developed countries, such as Argentina, Brazil, and India, industrial maritime powers with small navies (for example, Germany and Japan) might find it difficult to protect their interests with military power in the event of a violent confrontation. For the other major maritime forces—Britain, France, the United States, and the Soviet Union—each will still retain the ability to overcome these types of threats unless they occur in remote areas, such as the Straits of Magellan, in which case probably only the United States could engage in protracted operations against regional adversaries.

Although naval forces have a great deal of autonomy to operate in remote areas, fuel and ammunition supplies become critical constraints after a few days. These can be supplied by replenishment ships provided there is enough warning. There is little margin for error and very little redundancy in the system if a ship runs into serious difficulties. In other more accessible regions, the ability of the industrial maritime powers to overcome military threats is much greater. Although the local military powers may be able to raise the costs of any military engagement, they will ultimately be beaten. The ability to raise costs is, of itself, however, an important political weapon which might deter the industrial maritime force from asserting its rights under certain circumstances. For example, in 1971 the United States sailed the nuclear carrier *Enterprise* from the South China Sea through the Straits of Malacca into the Bay of Bengal to lend support to Pakistan in that country's war with India. At that time, the U.S. decision aroused resentment on the part of the littoral states, especially Singapore and Malaysia, which protested this operation. What might happen in the future if such an exercise were again attempted, this time with the implicit threat from a well-armed littoral state to deny access? Here again, the point is not that the United States would be unable to get through in extremis but that its political leadership might not consider the political costs worth the political benefits.

The growth of Soviet naval capabilities and those of smaller countries has been discussed in the context of their relationship to the West's growing dependency on sea lines of communications to carry its products and raw materials from point to point. It has been suggested in many quarters, including some within the U.S. Navy, that the possible interdiction of commercial sea lanes is a threat the West must take seriously in the future, and this will require a greater investment in sea control ships to protect Western merchantmen from a latter-day *guerre de course*, or commerce raiding. The idea that these raids could assume greater importance in the context of Western defense planning deserves careful examination.

The assumption behind the concept of *guerre de course* is that to destroy an enemy's seaborne commerce is, in effect, to destroy his capability to wage protracted warfare—if a high percentage of his economic welfare is based upon maritime trade. One of the most articulate advocates of the concept was Théophile Aube, who, in the late nineteenth century, founded the French *jeune école* of naval strategy. One purpose of Aube's strategy was to counter the emphasis prevalent throughout the Western world on the value of capital ships as the primary instruments of maritime power. The leading capital ship advocates drew many of their ideas from the writings of Mahan, whose major work, *The Influence of Sea Power Upon History*, had been published in 1890 and strongly advocated the capital ship. Aube and his associates argued that for a maritime power such as France, it was hopeless and counterproductive to try to match Britain in capital ship production. Instead, the weaker power should focus on building up a fleet for commerce raiding against the merchantmen of the major maritime power and hit at the heart of the adversary's economic system without confronting the enemy's main naval forces head-on.

Furthermore, Aube and his collegues believed that in the torpedo boat they had found the perfect giant killer. This weapons system, which was fast and lethal, would be deployed out of France's Channel ports, interdict British commerce in the Channel, and retreat to the French ports before the superior British fleet could be alerted. Such attacks would send shudders through the City of London before the Admiralty fully realized what was happening, and the City, the financial center of the British Empire, ultimately had more power than the Admiralty in Victorian England. To this extent, the raids on British commerce, rather than being a sideshow, would strike the adversary with particularly devastating effects.[4]

Although Aube's theory grossly overestimated the capabilities of motor torpedo boats, the submarine was initially grossly underestimated by the maritime powers. The most effective examples of the *guerre de course* in recent times were (1) the German U-boat campaigns against Britain and (2) the U.S. submarine campaign against Japan in World War II, which destroyed the Japanese economy and involved very little contact with the Japanese naval forces.

The Soviet Threat to Western
Oil Sea Lines of Communication

The Soviet Union faces major constraints in embarking on raids against Western commercial shipping unless it limits its operations to certain geographical areas in close proximity to the Soviet landmass; it limits its interdiction to once-and-for-all encounters; and it secures access to major base facilities in distant areas. Although the present disposition of the Soviet fleet is not a source of major concern in the context of a protracted commerce war at sea, this state of affairs could change in the future, perhaps dramatically, if the Soviet Union were to establish major facilities in Vietnam, Iran, and Southern Africa.

The U.S. Chief of Naval Operations, Admiral Thomas Hayward, testifying on maritime superiority before the Senate Armed Services Committee in March, 1979, drew attention to the confusion that has arisen concerning the use of the terms sea control and power projection as missions to be pursued in obtaining maritime supremacy. He asserted that keeping control over the sea lanes implies much more than keeping the sea lanes open in the World War II convoy sense, for, as he pointed out, one way to ensure sea control is to deny an adversary the ability to use his maritime forces against the sea lanes. This often requires offensive military operations that more readily, but not necessarily, fall under the heading of power projection.

Consider the oil sea lines of communication from the Persian Gulf to the Western industrial countries. Clearly, the ability of the Soviet Union and its surrogates to threaten seriously the security of the SLOC varies greatly along the length of the SLOC, for what is important is the security of oil shipments; without oil the SLOC per se is of no strategic value. What we are talking about is the need to protect oil coming from the Persian Gulf which, during part of its journey from the wellhead to final consumers, must be transshipped by tanker across at least two oceans. To emphasize protection of the oil SLOC without parallel concern for the protection of oil fields, collecting systems, and local and final terminal facilities would be to stress only part of the problem, and oil production—as distinct from oil SLOC protection—requires different types of defense.

To illustrate this further, consider the problem of protecting oil from Saudi Arabia destined for the United States. At present, much of this oil is pumped from the vast Garwah oil field in southeast Saudi Arabia. After it has been extracted from the ground by pumps, it flows along a series of pipes to a central collecting area where many of the more volatile by-products are extracted. From the collecting, separation, and stabilizer plants, it flows to the local terminal and refinery facilities at the port of Ras Tanurah on the Persian Gulf. Here some of the oil is stored, some is refined, and some is loaded directly onto the supertankers. The supertankers then sail down the Gulf through the Strait of Hormuz, across the Indian Ocean, along the east coast of Africa, around the Cape, and across the Atlantic to terminals in the Caribbean. There, the oil is offloaded and either refined or transshipped in smaller tankers to U.S. ports.

For analytical purposes, at least eight stages of the oil flow can be identified which, in military terms, provide an adversary with eight target sets: the oil fields, the collecting, separation and stabilizer plants, the local terminals, the transshipment in tankers within the Persian Gulf, the transshipment in tankers across the ocean, the offloading facilities in the Caribbean, the tankers in transit from the Caribbean to the United States, and the final U.S. terminals. Thus, if the Soviet Union occupied the Gulf, it could close the Strait of Hormuz or interdict the oil fields, collecting system, and local terminals, and the oil would not get to the United States no matter how superior our military capabilities were along the rest of the chain or SLOC.

Although this point might seem obvious, it is an important one in view of some of the more simplistic statements that are made concerning the threats to the sea lines of communication. In fact, the least vulnerable stage of the oil flow from the Gulf is currently the transoceanic stage. This could become more vulnerable if the balance of power at sea changed, but, as has been pointed out elsewhere, this would require major geopolitical shifts and changes on the landmass of Asia and Africa that would result in the construction of maritime bases along the littoral.

No sensible Western maritime strategy can be envisaged that does not also take into account the environment on the landmass from which most of the resources come. In the Persian Gulf, in the absence of an overall strategy for using military power in the Gulf, a forward-based U.S. maritime posture will not be used to cover some of the most likely military contingencies in the region and certainly not the most serious ones—namely, a Soviet invasion of the Gulf.

There is an important general lesson concerning maritime power to be applied to an analysis of the Gulf problem. The Gulf case demonstrates the close interplay between the maritime posture and the balance of power on the landmass. It suggests that a shift of the balance of land forces will have an important and perhaps decisive impact on the balance of maritime forces; and, in theory, it suggests that a position of maritime superiority could rapidly shift to one of maritime inferiority if control of the landmass were to change. Thus, although the United States currently has what would appear to be maritime superiority in the Persian Gulf-Indian Ocean region, primarily on account of its superior support facilities and maritime air capabilities, a Soviet military presence in Iran (or, for that matter, Saudi Arabia) could decisively change the balance; it would permit the Soviet Union a secure base in the Gulf and, in the case of Iran, direct land access to its southern borders. It would also permit the use of local air bases by Soviet naval aviation (SNA) aircraft, such as the Backfire B, which would compound threats to the U.S. fleet in the northwest quadrant of the Indian Ocean and in the Gulf itself. In fact, a Soviet presence in Iran would make any U.S. naval presence in the Gulf extremely risky in any shooting war. Similar radical changes in the maritime balance in the eastern Mediterranean would occur if Turkey were to withdraw from NATO or, in extremis, were to fall under Soviet control in a war or crisis.

One reason for stressing this close interrelationship between the land and maritime balance is to redress the tendency to talk of land and maritime forces as substitutes for one another. In reality, they complement each other for most of the critical war-fighting missions. Thus, in any serious Persian Gulf contingency whose goal is protection of oil supplies against a major attack, maritime forces would play a vital role in the early stages of the conflict; but the long-run control of the Gulf would more appropriately be assigned to ground and tactical air forces.

Exceptions to these conclusions would be cases where the United States could secure no land facilities and therefore would be forced to fight or intervene with maritime forces. In this case, a serious question would be the extent to which the U.S. maritime forces had ready access to supplies and other rear-based facilities.

Other Scenarios for a *Guerre de Course*

Where does this examination of the possibilities of a *guerre de course* involving the major powers lead to? There seem to be two possibilities in which attacks on merchant ships might occur and have important outcomes. The first would be in a regional war between small countries in the less developed world. The ability of one side to isolate, blockade, and interfere with maritime commercial operations would, depending on the countries in question, have a significant impact on a war. For example, if Singapore and Malaysia ever fought each other, and if Malaysia were able to close or control the Strait of Malacca and the approaches to the Singapore

Strait, it would pose an extremely serious threat to Singapore because the lifeblood of the nation would be threatened. A similar problem would face Taiwan or any of the smaller maritime powers which depend on freedom of access for their economic survival.

At the level of great power conflict, it is much less easy to imagine either smaller powers or the Soviet Union attacking Western commerce, except in the context of general war. In a general war, however, the issue could become very important, especially if it were thought possible that a nuclear war could extend into a broken-back phase and become essentially a war of attrition. Alternatively, if the Soviet Union had the conventional forces to fight a *guerre de course* against the West, it could put the West into the position of having to escalate to nuclear exchange or negotiate from weakness.

In conclusion, the emerging maritime environment suggests that under certain highly circumscribed circumstances commerce raiding could have a serious impact on the United States and its allies, and for this reason maritime supremacy should remain a primary mission for the United States and its allies. The notion that the USSR and its potential allies can deny the West resources by raiding its commerce is less plausible given the difficulty of mounting such an operation at sea. Thus, efforts to build naval forces to protect convoys might well detract from the more important role of deterring Soviet political military action around the periphery and on the landmass of Eurasia in areas such as the Gulf and the Horn of Africa.

NEW MARITIME TECHNOLOGIES

The development of new technologies with maritime applications has been nothing short of revolutionary over the past 20 years and could, over the next two decades, further alter our geopolitical dependence on access to areas such as the Persian Gulf. In this final section, we will examine only general technological trends as distinct from specific considerations of weapons systems. The list of technologies is impressive and covers everything from improvements in ship and hull design (exemplified by the supertanker, the bulk carrier, container ships, and, for the future, surface effects ships) to vastly improved propulsion and navigation systems, offshore technology for mining and exploration, and the exploration of outer space and its relationship to the maritime arena.

The impact of the supertanker and bulk carriers on maritime commerce has been far-reaching. The economies of scale made possible by such large vessels have helped to keep transportation costs down to a small percentage of the total costs of international trade between distant places. Furthermore, the speed of transit between points has greatly improved because of the ability of the new ships to travel intercontinental distances without refueling and because of their ability to sail through all but the most severe weather conditions. Thus supertankers from the Gulf and large container ships from Australia can reach North America with no need for port calls except in emergency. Although transit stops at convenient ports such as Cape Town (so-called "unauthorized" port calls) are still frequently made, they would not be necessary in wartime or crisis. Thus, the endurance of the modern transportation ships has increased despite the fact that they are still powered by conventional fuels. Similarly, although there have been several well-publicized occasions when the supertankers have foundered in adverse weather conditions, for the most part they are much easier to sail and navigate in inclement weather than were their predecessors. In other words, the sheer inhospitality of the Arctic and Atlantic environment to the convoys of

World War II would not be repeated today in the event of a major resupply in these areas.

The major revolution in propulsion has been nuclear power. So far, this has not proven economical for commercial fleets, although it is possible that this will change as fossil fuels become more expensive and improvements in nuclear power plants continue. The great advantage of the nuclear-powered ship is its ability to sail for years at high speeds without refueling. In theory, the marriage of nuclear propulsion and radical platforms, such as the air-cushion vehicle, could result in much faster ships operating at speeds of up to 100 knots. Such ships remain in the world of fantasy, however, primarily because of the excessive weight of contemporary nuclear engines.

Other changes in ship design that have had or will have fundamental implications for operations include the roll-on/roll-off concept, which means that ships contain their own off-loading capabilities and can therefore operate free from the normal constraints of ports. In military operations, these innovations have obvious merits, especially if deployments in underdeveloped regions of the world are envisaged.

Other new technologies in the commercial arena include methods that range from refrigerating fish on factory ships to the construction of gigantic oil platforms taller than the Empire State Building that can be operated in hurricane-force winds and in deep waters. Offshore oil and gas exploration and extraction account for most of the new technology, but there have also been some impressive breakthroughs in the technology for ocean mining.

Great improvements have also been made in the design and construction of large, super-stable, floating, semi-submersible concrete platforms upon which a myriad of economic activities can take place, including oil extraction, mining, and nuclear power generation. The impact of the offshore industry is much greater than the immediate product distribution would suggest. With oil and gas extraction, the associated industries have to include the support of offshore operations, which are widespread in areas such as the North Sea. Perhaps the most futuristic example of these technologies is the vast oil complex in the Norwegian sector of the North Sea that makes up what is known as Etofisk City; in reality, it is a series of concrete platforms used for oil pumping and oil storage that are connected by covered passageways.

Also important for maritime activities are the changes occurring in space technology. What space means for the maritime arena is only beginning to be appreciated, but over the next 30 years space surveillance and communications systems will become increasingly critical components of the nation's maritime posture. If the economic and military exploration of outer space continues, the relationship with the maritime environment will grow. Space has become to the sea what the airplane became in the 1930s and in World War II: an essential and integral element in the overall posture. Thus, today it is not possible to compare the naval capabilities of various countries unless one includes in the analysis a comparison of their respective maritime air capabilities; for without air power most naval forces have become vulnerable for all but peacetime presence missions.

The same logic applies to outer space. It is well documented that generations of senior naval planners in the major maritime countries ignored the importance of aircraft in influencing the nature of sea control. Today, because of restrictive perspectives on the nature and purpose of U.S. maritime strategy, we may run the risk of ignoring (or at least not fully appreciating) the potential that outer space has for maritime power. Although it is

APPROACHES TO THE
PERSIAN GULF REGION

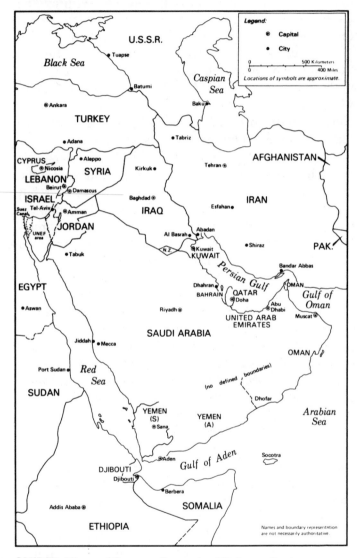

SOURCE: Library of Congress, Congressional Reference Service

true that the U.S. Navy has recognized the value of satellite communications and has accordingly invested large sums of money in outer space programs, it still has a somewhat parochial attitude toward the further exploration and settlement of outer space by the United States or, for that matter, the Soviet Union. One purpose of this section, therefore, is to suggest that just as Mahan emphasized the importance of the geographic configuration of the landmass in outlining his elements of sea power, so, today, we must emphasize the importance of outer space in calculating our maritime posture for the remainder of the century and beyond.

To state it another way, if the Soviet Union were to become the dominant space power in the next 30 years and establish the ability to control space in the event of international conflict, the implications for U.S. maritime power would be grave. If the Soviet Union could destroy U.S. satellites and protect its own, its ability to change the balance of power in terms of strategic nuclear exchange, power projection, sea control, and the operation of commercial maritime trade would be immense. Just as Douhet postulated that control of the air would revolutionize the land battle—and to that extent his theories were right—so it can be argued that control of space would radically alter the nature of the future land, sea, and air battles.

CONCLUSION

To survive the geopolitical threats posed by diminished maritime power and the increased need for maritime access, the Western industrial powers must adopt both short- and long-term policies to regain the superior global position they once had. While it is unrealistic to expect a return to the halcyon days of the 1950s and early

1960s, much can be done to redress the present and anticipated vulnerabilities. Above all, this requires strong and imaginative leadership and the willingness to exploit more actively the remaining assets the Western powers have — namely, superior technology and production capabilities. Technology is the answer not only to dependency on unique and vulnerable geographical areas such as the Persian Gulf, but also to the long-term challenges posed by the changing world environment and the increasingly adventurist policies pursued by the Soviet Union.

II. The Strait of Hormuz: Strategic Chokepoint

Robert J. Hanks and Alvin J. Cottrell

The advanced industrial societies of the West are hostage to many vital natural resources, significant portions of which are found primarily in the less developed countries of the globe. This dependence is increasing daily. Some partially advanced nations—South Africa, for instance—can boast ownership of either the bulk of the world's supply of selected minerals and metals or the major share of those lying outside Communist control. However, the importance of these commodities, indispensible to Western industrialized economies, is overshadowed at present by the critical position of the catalyst required to transform them into useful products. In 1980 the catalyst is petroleum. And, again, it is the Third World that possesses the major share of the global supply of oil.

The conventional distinction between advanced industrial nations and nations of the Third World is an imprecise concept. In practical terms, there are three worlds. The first comprises the most advanced countries and includes the United States, the nations of Western Europe, the Soviet Union, and the countries of Eastern Europe. To this core group one must also add Japan.

Though seldom referred to, there is a Second World. In it one finds those nations reasonably far along on the road to industrial status but still containing within their borders, to one degree or another, many of the critical problems of underdevelopment. This group encompasses a large number of countries, including Brazil, South Africa, Taiwan, Korea, and the People's Republic of China.

Finally, there is the much-publicized Third World, a wide range of new and old nations that exist at the lower end of the international economic spectrum with subsistence economies, largely illiterate populations, and often tribal social systems. Examples of this latter category include the nations of Central Africa, Southeast Asia, and Central America. The countries associating themselves with the nonaligned movement, although predominantly in this Third World category, are also joined by some in the second classification as well.

In the near term it is not potential shortages of metals and minerals from the Second and Third Worlds that pose the most immediate threat to economies in the First World. Without these materials, or significant fractions of the amounts currently imported, Western industrial societies would assuredly suffer. At the moment, however, the critical ingredient is a continuous supply of crude oil to allow raw materials to be converted into essential products. As in the case of metals and minerals, the bulk of the known global petroleum reserves lies within the borders of the Third World. Production of oil by what were considered the giants of the industry—the United States and the Soviet Union—began to decline a number of years ago as their huge fields suffered progressive depletion. Simultaneously, the share of the international market owned by other nations began to increase, until now, when countries such as Saudi Arabia, Kuwait, Iran, Nigeria, Libya, and Venezuela sit atop the majority of the known reserves. Saudi Arabia is clearly the Gargantua of the oil production business; when that nation's deposits are coupled with those of other Persian Gulf countries, the share of world reserves falling under their control approaches 60 percent.

Energy is the indispensible factor that makes the entire industrial process function. Because oil currently dominates all other sources of energy, a little-known stretch of salt water, the Strait of Hormuz, has assumed immense strategic importance. Through that narrow, maritime passage, separating Ras Musandam on the Arabian Peninsula and a corresponding indentation on the Iranian coastline at Bandar Abbas, tankers carry most of the Middle East petroleum so vital to Western economies. Despite recent construction of additional pipelines to transport Persian Gulf oil to the Mediterranean Sea, the overwhelming percentage of oil still leaves the Persian Gulf in ships. Whether they are comparatively small tankers, bound around the southern end of the Arabian Peninsula via the Red Sea for the Suez Canal, or the "Very Large Crude Carriers" (VLCC)—the familiar supertankers—that sail south around the Cape of Good Hope and eastward through the Indian Ocean to the Pacific, all of these ships must transit the confined waters of the Strait of Hormuz. On board are cargoes that provide 50 percent of the petroleum imported by the United States, 70 percent of that used by the nations of Western Europe, and 90 percent of that used by Japan. Clearly, this narrow shipping chokepoint is currently one of the most important bodies of salt water on the face of the globe.

Future technological progress will eventually unlock new sources of energy. It is conceivable, for instance, that before too long there will be a massive exploitation of solar power; the expansion of fission, along with the emergence of fusion power, may play a major role. Even with fission, however, we will have to hurry. Some analysts have postulated that fission reactors—based on known uranium supplies and built at a rate of three 1000-megawatt units per week between now and the end of the century—would meet only one-half of the growing energy demand in the world. The foregoing program would result in 3500 gigiwatts of nuclear-powered energy being generated by the year 2000. Yet, this would not be enough. Though failing to close the growing gap between supply and demand, this level of effort would nonetheless exhaust the world's known uranium reserves in the short space of 12 years.

In the years immediately ahead, the world confronts an energy crisis of immense proportions. Until an advancing technology can convert renewable sources of power from solar, fusion, the tides, and annual energy-producing crops, oil and coal, accompanied by conservation efforts, will have to serve the bulk of mankind's needs. As Second and Third World nations develop further, they will become competitors, along with the Soviet Union and Eastern Europe, for energy—petroleum in particular. Thus, until the energy problem is solved, the Strait of Hormuz will be perhaps the most important strategic point on the face of the planet. For this reason the world must be concerned about the waters that ebb and flow through the Strait, with events transpiring within the nations adjacent to it, and with the political realities that govern the waters beyond.

For the West there is another crucial consideration. We all live in a world of power politics. Nations are not governed—let alone populated—by Rousseau's perfect man, and nations are not altogether different from the fallible human beings that inhabit them. When one realizes that the Western world's foremost adversary, the Soviet Union, is rapidly exhausting its own domestic petroleum reserves, it follows that a major international conflict may well be in the making. The Strait of Hormuz could become the focus of that confrontation. Many observers believe that the Soviet invasion of Afghanistan is the first such move Moscow has made on the international energy chessboard.

THE HISTORICAL CONTEXT

Petroleum has been a prime necessity for mankind's existence only in the most recent decades, although its growing importance has been evident for about 100 years. Since the drilling of the first oil well at Titusville, Pennsylvania, in 1859, crude petroleum has steadily expanded its role in the energy spectrum. The United States—the pioneer in commercial production of oil—led the world in the exploitation of this new commodity. Furthermore, the conjunction of this event with the Industrial Revolution, which would transform the world at a geometric rate, served to accelerate what might otherwise have been an evolutionary development.

Prior to the technological explosion of the nineteenth century, national economics had been labor intensive. Goods and services were produced essentially by man or animal power. Exceptions to this rule were the use of the water wheel and the windmill, which allowed man to harness the energy in water and wind. With the advent of machines powered by other sources of energy, all that began to change. Coal combustion, coupled with James Watts's steam engine, irreversibly altered man's way of life. The discovery of oil transformed it even further, for it made possible the internal combustion engine. Ultimately, the latter development was destined not only to render man individually mobile at speeds far beyond those he could achieve afoot or on horseback, but eventually to free him from the gravitational bonds that had confined him to the surface of the earth.

From that early beginning in Pennsylvania, the search for sources of petroleum and new ways to exploit its remarkable potential went forward swiftly. No one could foresee at that time of expanding discoveries of oil deposits that the supplies of "black gold" were not inexhaustible and that, at the increasing rate of consumption being generated worldwide, the bottom of the oil barrel would be reached long before anyone could have anticipated.

As the imperatives of the industrial revolution exerted their pressures, the demand for oil grew. Coal, of course, continued for some time to power huge steam engines, driving ships and railroad trains as well as the burgeoning number of plants producing electricity. But as the internal combustion engine matured, it became obvious that this liquid fuel could supplant coal in heavy-engine applications and do so at great savings in manpower.

As the search for this new form of usable energy proceeded, geologists quickly recognized that the conditions existing in Pennsylvania must surely be duplicated, not only elsewhere in the United States but in various other parts of the world. Accordingly, the quest for new petroleum fields—employing the American-pioneered technology—spread around the globe. Even before World War I, exploratory drilling had reached the Middle East, where—as a result of the proliferation of petroleum drilling technology and expertise—an intense scramble among the more advanced industrial nations ensued. Middle Eastern prospects seemed sufficiently promising to justify comparatively heavy investment in the sinking of exploratory wells in the 1930s. It is clear today, however, that the experts in those early days failed to foresee the extent of the bonanza that initial discoveries in the deserts of Saudi Arabia would one day produce.

Of the nations fronting on the Persian Gulf, Iran was the first to produce petroleum in commercial quantities. The first oil was taken from the sands of Persia in 1911; by the late 1920s, when the initial Iraqi well was brought in, almost 200 wells were producing in Iran. Then, in 1931, the Americans—in the California-Texaco Oil Company (CALTEX)—brought their first, solely owned and operated well on line in Bahrain. The discoveries in these initial fields were immense when judged by the standards of those days, but they were destined to be dwarfed by findings yet to come in Kuwait and then in Saudi Arabia.

In Kuwait, the largest single reservoir so far discovered, was tapped when a drilling bit penetrated the incredibly prolific Burgan field near al Ahmadi, south of the city of Kuwait. The event coincided with the outbreak of World War II. To prevent Germany from gaining access to an operating field, producing the petroleum it needed for its huge military machine, Burgan No. 1 was shut down almost as soon as it was discovered. If the output of a well in Texas or Oklahoma can be increased from 15 to 25 barrels per day, it is considered a major achievement. Yet Burgan No. 1, now only one of a number of wells in the vast field, reactivated in the days immediately following World War II, without the aid of rocker-arm pumps (the reservoir was pressurized by entrapped, free natural gas) began spouting 25 *thousand* barrels of oil each day. In 1973, 35 years after its discovery and 25 years after it had been put into full production, it was still prducing petroleum at nearly the same rate.

In the years following World War II, additional discoveries in Saudi Arabia, Qatar, Abu Dhabi, and Dubai made it clear that the Persian Gulf was the world's foremost source of liquid energy. Of equal significance was the fact that the only maritime egress from the Gulf was an acutely constricted sea passage: the Strait of Hormuz. In those early days few people in the Western world—particularly in the United States—gave much thought to the Persian Gulf, let alone the Strait of Hormuz. Only a few people beyond the immediate region even knew the strait existed. The United States was still the world's largest producer of petroleum—certainly its premier exporter—and other sources were being discovered almost daily in Libya, Indonesia, Nigeria, Venezuela, and elsewhere. The supply of oil seemed limitless.

Furthermore, the mastery of nuclear fission had caused a quantum advance in technology during World War II. In the immediate postwar period the destructiveness of this new force was considered to be more than offset by its promise as an unlimited source of energy for mankind. No matter that petroleum supplies might be finite, uranium would take over before the oil reserves were depleted and solve the global energy problem.

Thus, two crucial myths were born: first, that the world might soon arrive at the outer boundaries of available energy; second, and of far greater importance, that there was no need to seek out and exploit alternative energy sources because of the overabundance of inexpensive oil and the infinite possibilities of nuclear energy. Consequently, the Strait of Hormuz remained unnoticed.

Closure of the Suez Canal in 1967 did little to alter the world's knowledge about or appreciation of the importance of the Persian Gulf. Western technology and industrial expertise merely stepped into the breach and produced the supertanker. The size of these ships captured the imagination and attention of the world, obscuring the fact that the apparently insatiable global appetite for petroleum was daily increasing the flow of oil through the Strait of Hormuz.

Nowhere in the world was this reality less remarked than in the United States, where, in the short space of ten years prior to 1967, America had shifted from being a net exporter of oil to being an importer of a significant portion of its annual petroleum consumption. In 1981, the United States looks to imports to meet nearly half of its daily needs, with a very large proportion of those imports coming from the Middle East via the Strait of Hormuz.

Two events in recent years have demonstrated the Western nations' heavy dependence upon oil from the Persian Gulf region. First, the Organization of Arab Petroleum Exporting Countries (OAPEC), at the time of the 1973 war, clamped a complete embargo on exports to the United States and the Netherlands. The United States had provoked Arab wrath by supporting Israel with an airlift of military equipment and the grant of $2 billion in additional aid. The Dutch were embargoed because their national airline, KLM, was discovered to have flown Jewish aircraft pilots into Tel Aviv to take part in the war.

Additionally, to exert further pressure on the United States, OAPEC instituted a series of petroleum production cutbacks that reduced the availablility of oil worldwide. This created an acute, albeit artificial, shortage of oil. Even though this particular shortage was clearly contrived, it should have signaled to all oil-importing countries that the balance of the world's supply rested on a thin edge and that any one of a number of events could produce precisely the same result: an oil cutoff.

OAPEC's reduction of supplies, coupled with pressures exerted primarily by Iran, Venezuela, and Indonesia (not OAPEC members but powers in the larger, global association, OPEC, the Organization of Petroleum Exporting Countries), caused the price of oil to sky-rocket. This sharp climb in the wellhead price of petroleum and an accompanying demand by producing states for increased participation—a euphemism for acquiring greater control over production from the foreign companies that had exercised de facto ownership of the wells and refineries from the outset—served to obscure the growing problem of global petroleum supply versus world demand. As in the development of the supertanker, the importance of the Strait of Hormuz was once again overlooked.

Five years later, in 1978-1979, a second and even more forthright indication that the day of energy reckoning was fast approaching was signaled by the revolution in Iran, which, among other things, brought that country's oil production to a complete halt for an extended period of time.

The narrow balance of petroleum supply and demand and the West's dependence on Middle Eastern oil was dramatically demonstrated when loss of production from the Iranian fields and refineries created an immediate global shortage. Unlike the crisis of 1973-1974, the shortage was not contrived; it was real, and it stemmed from events over which none of the importing countries had any semblance of control. Moreover, the margin of energy surplus was clearly shown to be thin, inasmuch as no nation except Saudi Arabia had spare capacity to make up for the loss of Iranian production. Even the Saudi reserve pumping and refining capacity was wholly inadequate to provide all of the six million barrels per day demanded by loss of the Iranian output. Despite the relatively small role Iranian oil then played in the U.S. energy picture, the sudden deficit nonetheless caused havoc at American gasoline pumps and some degree of panic in industry and among consumers.

After the 1973 embargo and the accompanying production slowdowns, the Iranian crisis and its effect on the world oil market should have signaled danger. By this time there should have been little doubt that the global energy picture was increasingly unsettled and that extraordinary measures needed to be taken to avoid crippling shortages and confrontations in the future over this shrinking resourse.

It bears repeating, however, that it was the impact of the shortages that caught the world's attention and focused that attention on essentially extraneous factors. In the United States there were few people who recognized that the relationship between petroleum demand and known supplies was approaching a critical stage; that the balance was so delicate that even a minor dislocation could cause serious global difficulties. Instead, the major, U.S.-controlled international oil companies were blamed for shortages at the gasoline pumps and the feared home heating oil deficits. The simplistic charge was that these companies were withholding supplies to force the price of petroleum products still higher, and once they obtained those price increases, oil would flow again.

At the same time, the oil weapon was brandished by Libya's Colonel Mu'ammar Qadhafi, who threatened to halt all production of oil unless Western countries rallied to the support of the Palestine Liberation Organization (P.L.O.). Almost simultaneously, Nigeria expropriated British Petroleum's holdings in that country and seized a BP oil tanker on the grounds that the company had surreptitiously diverted Nigerian oil to the Republic of South Africa. Then, joining the Libyan campaign, Nigeria circulated rumors that it would cut off all oil exports to the United States unless that country altered policies concerning the Palestinian issue and the Egyptian-Israeli negotiations following the Camp David agreements. Washington, beset with the effects of the shortage and the clamorous domestic demand for action, viewed this threatened further reduction in imports with something less than equanimity.

Thus, primary attention was once more riveted to the fact of a shortage and to peripheral, often irrelevant, factors rather than to the geographic aspects of the shortfall. The importance of the Strait of Hormuz was again lost in the background noise.

As a result, few people understood that every one of the exacerbating effects of the Iranian shutdown could be duplicated should passage through the Strait of Hormuz be interrupted or stopped altogether—something that could be achieved by any number of methods. Moreover, insofar as the U.S. and Dutch embargoes and accompanying production cutbacks were concerned, only a portion of the normal flow had been halted. Blockage of the Strait, of course, would cut off the oil completely. It is not terribly difficult to envisage what this would mean to the entire world..

The foregoing is valid only if the West is indeed hostage to the Middle East's energy sources. If the West can rely on alternate sources in times of shortage, crisis, or war— if there is a viable secondary source reasonably close at hand—the Strait immediately loses most of its significance.

THE ENERGY WORLD TODAY

In 1981 the world is in the uncomfortable position of being critically dependent upon a commodity that is swiftly being depleted and the bulk of which is controlled by a few. The 57.5 billion barrels of oil owned by the United States and its Western European allies constitutes but 8.1 percent of the world's 1979 proven oil reserves.

Furthermore, the countries that possess the lion's share of those reserves—essentially those bordering the Persian Gulf—cannot possibly spend the revenue from current production as rapidly as it accumulates. They therefore have no real incentive to increase production to meet growing international demands. More and more frequently, these producing countries claim their own national interests dictate that they produce petroleum only at rates necessary to meet their current budget requirements, including funding for modernization and industrialization programs. They believe it would be far better for them to conserve what in almost every case is their sole natural resource—excess production is infinitely more valuable to them in the ground than it is in tanker hulls. It is difficult to argue with the contention that it is wiser to let portions of a finite resource remain untapped, thus appreciating as the commodity becomes increasingly scarce, rather than to produce it at a maximum rate now and invest the revenue in a depreciating currency such as the U.S. dollar.

There is, of course, another side to that argument, and Saudi Arabia has acknowledged it both verbally and by its actions. Should the desert kingdom cut back petroleum production in accordance with the foregoing philosophy, a global recession—if not a depression—would probably result. The secondary impact on social and economic progress in Saudi Arabia would be profound, especially in light of that nation's huge investment of petrodollars in Western countries. To some extent the latter factor explains Riyadh's recent action to raise production about a million barrels per day above planned figures. In the wake of the Iran-Iraq war, Saudi Arabia raised production to 10.3 million barrels a day, the highest level in recent years.

Despite dramatic warning signals in the past few years, the fact that there really is a worldwide energy problem is only now being driven home to millions of people. Conservation efforts have slackened demand to some extent. At the same time, a few new sources have been discovered and are being brought on line. Most notable among the latter are the North Slope fields of Alaska, the North Sea fields that are now producing primarily for European consumption, encouraging discoveries in Mexico, China, and Angola. To be sure, other petroleum reservoirs surely exist; in the years ahead, some will probably be found and put into commercial production. It seems highly unlikely, however, that anything approaching the magnitude ofthe present Middle Eastern fields will be uncovered. Thus, until alternate sources of energy are brought on line, petroleum will continue to be the prime energy source for Western industrial nations, and dependence on the Persian Gulf fields will, at the very least, persist, and will most probably increase. In such circumstances, the Strait of Hormuz will remain crucial.

Furthermore, the period of that dependence will probably be somewhat longer than had heretofore been expected. The leading candidate to replace petroleum— nuclear fission—has suffered severe setbacks in recent months, particularly in the United States following the accident at Three Mile Island in Pennsylvania. The current U.S. administration's policy with respect to breeder reactor development suggests that the United States will have to be prepared to live within the limits of global uranium resources. Other nations—particularly the Soviet Union and France—may not be so reluctant. Even so, the worldwide future of fission reactors is constrained by the limitations of usable uranium and the campaigns of environmentalists.

Yet another energy alternative, fusion technology, is one of the major uncertainties in the present equation. It is impossible at the current stage of fusion development to forecast the future of this sort of power. One can only assume that man will one day master the techniques of harnessing fusion reactions, just as he did with fission.

Coal, of course, is likely to become an increasingly important source of energy, regaining a measure of the stature it enjoyed in the past. South Africa is the world leader in converting coal to oil and its other by-products. The South African Coal, Oil, and Gas Corporation (SASOL) process is well advanced, and the pilot plant—SASOL I—has become a money-making proposition in the wake of skyrocketing natural petroleum prices. SASOL II began production in early 1980, and when SASOL III—on which construction has just begun—is completed, South Africa will have gone a long way toward energy independence despite the fact that no natural petroleum has ever been discovered within its borders. Countries such as the United States, which boast huge coal reserves, can be expected to move in this direction as well. But even with the technology in hand today, nearly a decade is required to put one of these coal-conversion plants into full production.

A second possible method of obtaining oil from coal—direct liquification—will demand metallurgical techniques well beyond the boundaries of current knowledge. The prospects of other forms of energy production are not much different. Solar power research is still in its infancy, as is that for tidal power and geothermal sources.

Mankind has failed to recognize the limits of petroleum reserves and has ignored the geometrically increasing rates at which they are disappearing. As a result, it has been extremely tardy in seeking alternatives to black gold and in learning to conserve those amounts yet remaining. Other conclusions can also be drawn:

(1) For the foreseeable future, petroleum will continue to be the prime source of energy.

(2) As proven petroleum reserves are progressively depleted, control of the region where the largest remaining reserves are located—the Persian Gulf—will probably be contested by those nations hostage to its resources. In view of U.S. Central Intelligence Agency reports citing declining production in the USSR and expanding Eastern European demand, one of those contestants can be expected to be the Soviet Union.

(3) The strategic importance of the Strait of Hormuz, chokepoint through which the bulk of Middle Eastern oil will continue to flow, can be expected to increase rather than diminish. Almost inevitably, its waters will figure prominently in any struggle for control of Persian Gulf oil.

For all of these reasons, it is essential that the West acknowledge the unpalatable fact of the worldwide energy crisis and the role Middle Eastern petroleum will continue to play until one or more alternate energy sources can assume the burden. Guaranteeing Western access to Persian Gulf oil fields must include assuring free maritime passage through the Strait of Hormuz. For, notwithstanding the 1975 reopening of the Suez Canal and the subsequent construction of additional pipelines across the Arabian deserts to the shores of the mediterranean, the vast preponderance of oil leaving the Middle East will continue to exit the Persian Gulf via the Strait. It is no exaggeration to state that whoever controls these waters will have the ability to regulate the destinies of myriad nations, particularly those of the industrialized countries of the First World.

POLITICAL CHANGES
IN THE PERSIAN GULF

Perhaps the greatest threat to the interests of the United States and other large industrial powers is the political instability in the Persian Gulf region, because political instability threatens access to Persian Gulf oil. We often read about plans to protect the sea oil lines from the Persian Gulf, and there is no doubt that such concerns are more serious in the area of the Strait of Hormuz than anywhere else in the world. This is true because 30 percent of the world's oil production flows through the Gulf—only 600 miles in length from the Musandam peninsula (Oman) to Abadan (Iran) at the head of the Gulf—and because nowhere on the great Cape sea route extending around the African continent is there more potential and actual political instability. The concern here is the threat this instability poses to the regimes in the oil-producing countries, an instability that has taken hold in Iran, where, since the end of the monarchy, oil production has dropped from about six million barrels per day to about one million barrels or less.

Internal political instability in the Gulf can thus result in the limiting of oil production through slowdowns in production or sabotage in the area. In Khuzistan province, where Iran's oil fields are located, the population is largely composed of an Arab minority of three million people. They are a constant source of unrest and can easily be provoked to interrupt the production of oil.

What happened in Iran could happen in the Arab states of the Gulf. One of the great political weaknesses of the region is the system of government. Until 1958 the Gulf was ruled entirely by traditional and royal rulers: three kings, ten shaikhs or emirs, and one sultan. In 1958 a revolution occurred in Iraq in which the Hashemite kingdom was overthrown and the monarch, King Faisal, was assassinated. Then began a movement against royal or quasi-royal rule in the Gulf. In 1979 in Iran the second monarchy fell, leaving only Saudi Arabia with a royal family. Now part of the littoral of the Gulf is in the hands of rulers who are neither royal nor traditional. Such developments, however satisfactory they may be for the people of the area, do not ensure stable conditions for the production and export of oil. Any political change in the government of Saudi Arabia is not likely to be as favorable for the industrial powers, especially the United States, as is the current royal regime. Even changes within the monarchy could weaken our supporters. A political change would not have to be one hostile to the United States; it could merely be one in which the government decided to produce only the requisite oil to meet Saudi requirements rather than enough to assist the economy of the United States.

Should the monarchy fall in Saudi Arabia, all the small shaikhdoms of the United Arab Emirates, as well as Qatar, Bahrain, and Kuwait, would fall. The sultan of Oman, unless supported by the United States, probably would not last long. The sultan was in serious trouble in 1974 as a result of a Soviet-supported insurgent movement in Dhofar province that operated from a sanctuary in South Yemen. The rebellion was defeated only by a combination of British advisers, Jordanian military support, and 3500 troops dispatched at the sultan's request by the shah of Iran. Who would defeat a similar movement now if it were supported by the Soviets, their Cuban and East German surrogates, and the strong South Yemen armed forces? In short, traditional rule in the region may be short-lived—perhaps five to ten years at best.

The most powerful state to emerge in the area since the almost total decimation of the Iranian armed forces is the radical socialist state of Iraq, which—largely out of necessity—has been closely aligned with the Soviet Union since the overthrow of the Hashemite kingdom in 1958. Iraq's military strength, based on current estimates, is roughly 217,000 men. Total Iraqi forces at this writing are 185,000 in the army, 4000 in the navy, and 28,500 in the air force. Equipment is quite sophisticated in both the army and air force, and the troops have had substantial experience in fighting against their own Kurdish minority from the early to the mid-1970s.

Although Iraq has only a small navy, it is equipped with a number of fast Soviet missile boats that could be an important naval force in a small body of water such as the Gulf where its opponents—with the exception of Iran—are even more lightly armed. Indeed, Iraq's navy may be superior to the Iranian navy now in many respects, because its equipment is less sophisticated and thus easier to handle than that of the Iranians, who have lost most of their naval personnel—especially officers—capable of operating the more sophisticated weaponry procured under the shah's regime.

The revolution that wracked Iran in early 1979 drastically reduced its military capabilities in the region. From a total of about 430,000 men in all services, probably little more than 25 percent remain, and these are mostly junior officers, noncommissioned officers, and enlisted men. Nearly all high-ranking officers were shot, have retired, or fled the country. Thus, there will be a long period of rebuilding to reconstitute the Iranian armed forces, and there will be no real political stability in Iran until a disciplined Iranian armed force exists. The Iran-Iraq war has demonstrated that Iraq's forces are more effective for ground warfare. They have penetrated deeply into Iranian territory in the Khuzistan area, and Iran has not been able to organize an effective counterattack because of the decimation of the Iranian army command structure.

The emerging political situation may not be favorable to the United States or the West because it will depend on the outcome of Iran's internal political struggle. If leftist elements eventually take over the political system, they may seek Soviet support for rebuilding the armed forces. Iran could then act as a Soviet surrogate in harassing the sea lanes of the Gulf. Iran, we must remember, has sovereignty over 600 miles of coastline from the top of the Persian Gulf, along the eastern shore of the Strait of

Hormuz, to about 300 miles below the Strait along the Gulf of Oman. Thus, the political revolution in Iran may have still more serious results for the United States than merely the loss of Iranian oil. Iran may well become a more active military threat to the security of our oil interests in the entire region if leftists turn to the Soviets for military training and assistance. The chance that they will turn to the United States seem slight. The best the United States can hope for is that Iran will ask Western Europe for assistance.

Now that the system of royal rule is deteriorating throughout the Gulf, there is also a greater threat of military action between local states, which could also be a serious threat to oil production and oil exports, as the Iraq-Iran war demonstrates. Before the fall of the monarchy in Iran, only Iraq had a leftist government, and Iran and Iraq had many border clashes—many originating because of a lack of common political customs. Even the two large kingdoms, Iran and Saudi Arabia, had many differences, but conflict between them was less likely because of their common form of government. This was also true of the other shaikhdoms and the Sultanate of Oman. They all had a stake in the survival of traditional rule, which tended to overshadow other potential sources of conflict. All this is now eroding, and it is likely that conflict will increase in the area as the states begin to act with little regard for the political forms of government. Meanwhile, differences in their political systems are likely to create conflict until all royal rule disappears.

In the years since 1935, when significant oil production began in this area, the West dominated the littoral states, and the limited but symbolically important British military presence in the region patrolled and protected the area. The United States, which in a sense replaced the British presence at the time of the British withdrawal from east of Suez on November 30, 1971, has really never had to worry about the security of the sea lanes to and from Hormuz, because all the states were in the hands of traditional rulers left in the wake of Britain's departure. Even in the United Arab Emirates (U.A.E.), which consist of the seven former shaikhdoms of Trucial Oman in the southern Gulf, there had been stability as a result of British influence in commercial and military affairs, a stability that continued after Britain's withdrawal. British bankers, administrative officers, and military men occupied the key positions in this area. This situation is now deteriorating, and more and more of these positions will inevitably be occupied by local Arab leaders who will, quite understandably, wish to exercise their own authority. The new leaders will be influenced by those who do not want traditional rule, and the whole structure of government will most likely give way, not necessarily to better rule, but at least to new, nontraditional forms of political rule.

The political changes on the shores of the Gulf will increasingly determine the amount of oil produced as well as the security of the sea lanes on which it is shipped. It will make very little difference in the West's ability to protect the sea lanes beyond the Gulf if the producing states of the Gulf decide to restrict or cut off the amount of oil reaching the sea lanes.

Any change in the political leadership of Oman that weakens the rule of the sultan would pose serious threats to the transit of Gulf oil. Oman is not important as an oil-producing state; its importance lies in its control of the easternmost tip of the Musandam peninsula that juts out to within seven miles of the outbound supertanker lane in the 21-mile-wide Strait of Hormuz. This outbound lane is about four to five miles wide, and ships can easily be reached by artillery or missiles fired from the tip of the Omani peninsula. This promontory is separated from Oman proper by two shaikhdoms of the U.A.E. that bisect the peninsula below the tip of the cape. The cape is already vulnerable to hostile forces because of this geographic separation, but if the sultan were overthrown by those antiroyal forces behind the Dhofar rebellion—the Popular Front for the Liberation of Oman—the Strait and the more than 1000 miles of coastal waters of Oman would become even more vulnerable.

Another serious threat to free passage through the Strait is the unrest in a non-Gulf country, Pakistan, whose Baluchistan province borders on the Gulf of Oman at the strait's 200-mile-wide southern approaches. Many young Baluchi students seek either some autonomy or complete independence from Islamabad. There has been a long-standing claim for greater autonomy on the part of the Baluchi tribal chiefs, and this claim is being pursued aggressively now by younger Baluchi students since the Soviet invasion of Afghanistan. Some of these students seem willing to accept Soviet help. If an independent Baluchistan could be established, one might credibly expect the leaders of such an entity to aid the Soviets either by granting them a naval base on the Gulf of Oman or the Arabian Sea, or by engaging in harassment of the sea lanes to and from the Persian Gulf. Thus, political changes in the region could well presage much greater threats to U.S., Western, and Japanese oil interests in the area than have hitherto seemed credible. A serious question is whether or not the United States and the West can cope with these threats. Clearly, in the case of Oman, giving the sultan our unqualified political support and providing him with military assistance is absolutely vital. U.S. military guarantees may also be necessary. To only a slightly lesser extent, the same is true for Pakistan, whose strategic position is also critical to the security of the approaches to the Strait of Hormuz.

The United States must also attempt to improve commercial and diplomatic relations with Iraq, because Iraq may represent a political trend in the region and is already militarily the most important Gulf state. After

NOTE: Persian Gulf at left; Gulf of Oman at right. Oman, Musandam peninsula at bottom. Iranian coastline, island of Qeshm at top.
SOURCE: National Aeronautics and Space Administration.

Strait of Hormuz

Saudi Arabia, it is also the Gulf's most important oil-
producing state.

VULNERABILITY OF SHIPPING
TRANSITING THE STRAIT OF HORMUZ

There are many points at which the movement of Middle Eastern oil could be interrupted if someone, a group,
or a nation should determine to do so. Starting at the

wellhead, through the collection stations to storage and refinery facilities, thence to the loading docks, through the complex network of interconnecting pipelines, the flow of this critical fuel could be disrupted before it ever departs the country of origin. For those cargoes destined for the United States and Western Europe, there are three oceans to cross, and, at the end of the voyage, other facilities could be considered targets. Each of these points is vulnerable.

Ships traveling the saltwater highways of the world also confront other dangers to their safety—some natural and some manmade. Every competent mariner can enumerate the perils posed by nature: the weather, restricted and shallow water, and peculiar maritime phenomena that so often result from a combination of these elements. For example, the killer or freak wave periodically encountered off the eastern coast of South Africa between Durban and Cape Agulhas—the southernmost tip of the African continent—has sunk numerous ships, including some of the largest oil tankers in service. Familiar, too, are the effects of Indian Ocean cyclones, Pacific typhoons, and Atlantic hurricanes on ships at sea.

To these dangers man has added a rather extensive list of his own that can be categorized along a conflict continuum, running from relative peace to full-scale warfare. At the lower end of this spectrum are threats posed by pirates, who seek monetary gain, and terrorists, who generally pursue political objectives. Further along the scale are threats mounted by nations themselves. Here the variety of action is likely to be greater in that it can include operations of local naval forces, attacks delivered from land bases by aircraft or by shorter-ranged weaponry employed in particularly narrow waterways, and surreptitious provision of support or haven by a nation to those actually mounting the attack. Finally there is a major war, wherein all of the maritime forces of the belligerents are engaged. In these circumstances, neutral shipping usually pays a very heavy price as well. The massive maritime campaigns of World War I and II offer abundant testimony to the dangers seaborne traffic confronts at this end of the conflict spectrum.

In this analysis, however, the central focus is on a single, critical, maritime chokepoint: the Strait of Hormuz. Thus, we will confine our discussion to those threats that can endanger shipping—mercantile or naval—moving through these constricted waters. Although the primary issue is the safety of oil tankers making their way in and out of the Persian Gulf, one must examine other maritime problems, including those faced by naval commanders whose forces must operate in and around the Strait. Perhaps the best point of departure for such an examination lies at the lower end of the conflict spectrum.

Piracy and Terrorism

Piracy was once a flourishing activity in the Persian Gulf region. In particular, the shaikhdom of Ras al-Khaimah—now part of the U.A.E.—not so long ago was the home of the largest and most feared group of pirates in the area. Piracy was eventually stamped out by Great Britain through the efforts of the Royal Navy and the British East India Company. Following negotiation of a series of nineteenth-century treaties between London and the local shaikhs, the Pirate Coast became known as the Trucial Coast.

Piracy, of course, has not been wholly eliminated. It still persists throughout Southeast Asia, especially in the Indonesian archipelago, and it appears from time to time elsewhere around the globe. In November 1978 a band of knife-wielding pirates boarded an Argentinian freighter in the port of Palmas in the Canary Islands but were driven off by crewmen armed with rifles. In the vicinity of the Strait of Hormuz piracy no longer is a significant problem, although, as elsewhere, it has not disappeared completely. Today, the practice is confined mainly to the dhow traffic and poses no real threat to the tankers transiting the Strait, although it cannot be ruled out completely. The terrorist threat, of course, is a different matter.

Nations of the world are painfully familiar with the problem of terrorism as it has affected air traffic. For a time, hijacking of commercial airliners reached epidemic proportions, forcing international action and coordination to combat it. Despite enormous effort, the practice has not been halted, and the seizure of airliners still occurs. The terrorist threat to commercial airliners manifests itself in a number of ways. Some aircraft have been seized and the plane and passengers eventually released. Other aircraft have been blown up on the ground. Still others have been shot down while approaching or departing airports.

The same perils lie in wait for commercial shipping. During the 1973 Arab-Israeli war, terrorist groups let it be known that American merchant ships in the Middle East, including oil tankers, would be targeted for destruction. They also threatened to hijack one or more U.S. ships.

Although it is not widely known, there have been fairly recent instances of ships being hijacked. In 1974 a terrorist group seized a merchantman in the harbor of Karachi, Pakistan, held the officers and crew hostage, and threatened to blow up the ship at the pier unless their demands were met. In 1975, two American antiwar activists, having infiltrated the crew of an American merchantman carrying a cargo of ammunition destined for Vietnam, took over the ship and forced the captain to sail it into Cambodian waters.

Given the realities of the Arab-Israeli confrontation, terrorist attacks against shipping transiting the Strait of Hormuz are a distinct possibility. PLO member Ibrahim Souss was extremely frank when asked recently if the PLO might consider attacks against tankers in the Strait of Hormuz. "Why not? The oil weapon is like any other weapon and we are at war."

Several possibilities quickly come to mind. First, of course, is the danger of a tanker being seized as it passes through these narrow waters. One can envision a motorized dhow lying in wait, several crewmen armed with shoulder-fired, antiaircraft rocket launchers of the Soviet Strella variety. There are a number of ways to let the captain of an outward-bound tanker know that unless he stops his ship and permits a party to come on board, he can expect several of these rockets to be fired into his thin-skinned ship—and it is not difficult to predict his reaction.

Consider, too, the likely response of a ship's captain when he is informed by a terrorist who has shipped as part of his crew that the loaded tanker is ringed with limpet mines equipped with time-delay fuses placed while it lay alongside the pier at Ras Tanurah taking on its volatile cargo. What is the captain's reaction when told that unless he stops the ship and permits a terrorist crew to come aboard, the mines will detonate at some undisclosed time?

It is a fairly simple process to devise other equally feasible methods a determined crew of hijackers could use to take over one of these huge ships. It would make little difference what the terrorists ultimately did with the ship. The first thing that would surely happen would be the termination of sailings through these waters until the owners were sure this sort of danger would not again be encountered. Looking at the Indian Ocean today, it becomes uncomfortably clear that naval forces adequate to guarantee the safety of these vulnerable ships are not readily available.

What if the terrorists decide that, rather than seize a ship, they would sink one? Here the possibilities are equally varied. The motorized dhow again provides an ideal vehicle. Under cover of darkness, the terrorists need only drop a few floating mines over the side in the path of an outbound tanker to achieve the requisite damage. The restricted maneuverability of these mammoth ships makes it highly likely that mines could be cast into the sea in broad daylight, and the bridge watch—even if it spotted them—would be unable to take evasive action in time to avert catastrophe. Then, there is always the threat of attack by missile launcher.

The problem presented by the mere announcement that the eight-mile-wide channel had been mined cannot be ignored. Ship owners would probably refuse to allow movement of their ships through these waters until they had been swept and certified free of mines. The extended disruption of oil supplies would be enormous.

That the threat of mining can cause infinite problems for shippers was abundantly demonstrated during World War II. German aircraft, flying at night, dropped concrete blocks—real mines were not available—in the Thames River estuary. British air-defense radar detected the aircraft as well as the fact that they were sowing something in those critical waters, but were unable to distinguish between mines and large chunks of cement. As a result, the port of London was abruptly closed and remained so for several weeks while a mine-sweeping operation was conducted. Ultimately, divers were sent down who discovered the hoax, and the port was reopened to shipping.

It is not inconceivable that the same sort of hoax could happen in the Strait of Hormuz without mines actually being planted. A declaration that mining had taken place would be enough to create severe interruption in the entire flow of oil from the Persian Gulf—a far more significant disruption than the stoppage of four million barrels per day that ensued in the wake of the Iranian revolution.

National Threats in the Region

The terrorist threat must be taken seriously and the threat from neighboring countries has to be taken into account as well. A little-known geographical fact, coupled with a local insurrection, could make the Strait of Hormuz one of the world's most vulnerable stretches of water. Although the Strait itself is many miles wide, the channel through which shipping passes is not. Moreover, outbound traffic hugs the shore of the Musandam peninsula, placing it within range of even the most unsophisticated weaponry on that spit of land. Artillery fire—not to mention missiles from modern launchers—can easily reach ships transiting the Strait. And anyone who has sailed in the vicinity of supertankers has to acknowledge that they make very large and inviting targets. It would be almost impossible to miss one at short range.

Although the tip of the Musandam peninsula is separated from the rest of the Sultanate by shaikhdoms of the U.A.E., it is nonetheless Omani territory. The current insurgency in Oman is centered in the far western Omani province of Dhofar, but Oman's ownership of the peninsula may explain the dedicated Soviet support of the rebellion and the equally strong fears of Great Britain, Jordan, and Iran that it might succeed.

The insurgency began under the rule of the present sultan's father, the xenophobic archreactionary, Said bin

Taimur, who had ruled the country since 1932. In 1962, a group of dissidents in Dhofar formed a liberation movement, and, by 1964, small-scale insurgent operations had begun to plague the sultan. Over the years, the rebellion grew in strength, and Marxist radicals gradually moved into positions of leadership. Backed with money and weaponry provided by the Soviet Union and funneled mainly through Moscow's South Yemeni surrogate, the Popular Front for the Liberation of Oman—a name subsequently changed to include the "Occupied Arab Gulf"—made slow but steady progress against the poorly trained and ill-equipped forces of the Sultan.

On July 24, 1970, Qaboos ibn Said—only son of the sultan—staged a bloodless palace coup, clearly aided and abetted by the British, who had long been firmly entrenched in the country. Banishment of Said and the swift institution of many domestic reforms by Qaboos did not, however, dampen the determination of the rebels of Dhofar. Sensing a chance to take over the entire country, they simply redoubled their efforts.

As interested in seeing the rebels defeated and the young sultan remain on the throne as the Soviets were to see just the opposite, Great Britain moved quietly to shore up the Omani defenses. Over the next few years, London was aided by Amman and Tehran, which contributed combat forces. With this assistance, Sultan Qaboos succeeded in ending the rebellion and capturing most of its leaders by 1975.

It is fairly easy to understand the strong Soviet support for the Dhofari rebels. It is also clear why the other nations came to the sultan's aid to forestall any threat to the oil traffic passing through those waters. It had escaped no one's attention that the Aden government had only recently buried tanks in the sands of Perim Island, which commands the equally narrow gateway to the Red Sea, and threatened to close the strait to any shipping to which it objected. Tanks had actually fired on a French freighter negotiating the channel past Perim Island. Great Britain, Jordan, and Iran's shah wanted to prevent this kind of control of the Strait of Hormuz by a radical government.

It is not surprising, therefore, that one of the first international consequences of the Iranian revolution can be perceived in Oman. No longer can Sultan Qaboos count on Tehran's help should the Dhofor rebellion be rekindled. Not only has the Ayatollah Ruhollah Khomeini renounced any Iranian military role in policing the waters in and around the Persian Gulf—an abrupt reversal of the shah's policy—but he has effectively reduced the Iranian army to impotence because he viewed it as a threat to the establishment of his own power. At the time of the shah's downfall, experienced observers predicted that one of the first external effects of the Iranian upheaval would be reactivation of the radical drive in Dhofor, this time with new leadership and, possibly, aid and advice from Cubans and East Germans. Without the kind of aid Sultan Qaboos has received in the past, it is altogether possible—indeed, probable—that the outcome of any renewed insurgency would be quite different.

On the other side of the Strait, the Iranian revolution continues, and the outcome is still far from clear. The revolution most assuredly did not end upon the return of Ayatollah Khomeini to Iran. The disparate groups that joined together under the anti-shah banner are now seeking different results, and the struggle for power goes on. Should some form of Marxist government triumph, ships passing through the Strait could be controlled in the same manner as they would if Dhofori rebels manage to overthrow Sultan Qaboos in Oman.

From Iran, threats would be far more varied and sophisticated. Despite Khomeini's cancellation of billions of dollars in arms purchases negotiated by the shah, the Iranian armed forces still boast considerable quantities of powerful, modern weapons. They have already begun to talk with other countries about their need for spare parts and technical assistance to keep extant systems in operation. Should they succeed, an Iran in radical Marxist hands could threaten shipping in the Strait of Hormuz with air attacks from nearby bases—attacks delivered by some of the most advanced aircraft in the world. The Iranian Navy, equipped with a number of small, fast, missile-armed patrol craft and a covey of hovercraft, also could significantly threaten commercial shipping in these waters. With this sort of weaponry, there would be little reason for Iran to depend on artillery pieces firing from the shore. Mining of the Strait would constitute yet another option for them.

Of course, the ultimate political orientation of Iran is as much if not more of a mystery than is the future of Sultan Qaboos. In part, the answers will depend heavily on the aspirations and actions of the Soviet Union. Like other traditional rulers in the region, Sultan Qaboos is firmly convinced that Moscow has grand designs on the region, based on Soviet machinations in Iraq, South Yemen, Ethiopia, Iran, and Afghanistan. The commitment of British, Jordanian, and the shah's armed forces to help Qaboos was evidence that those countries shared the sultan's fears.

The problem today is that the Strait of Hormuz is essentially unguarded. The shah is gone, and although Oman now has one of the better armed forces in the region, it is small and inadequately equipped. Without external help, Qaboos probably could not have succeeded in defeating the Dhofar rebels, small in number though they were. If there is a renewal of the revolt, the sultan's chances of quelling it are slim. With this situation in Oman, and the uncertain future of the Iranian revolution, local threats to the waterway are a real possibility. Insofar as the United States and its Western allies are concerned, emergence of a Marxist government on either side of the Strait would amount to the same thing: a Soviet-directed threat to the Western world.

Should there be open warfare, especially involving the two superpowers, the waters of the Strait of Hormuz would be less important than the littoral areas of the Strait and the Persian Gulf. In wartime the oilfields and associated installations would be the primary focus, just as they were during World War II.

During that war, when Hitler appeared capable of marching through North Africa, the Balkans, and the southern part of the Soviet Union into the Middle East—ostensibly to link up with the forces of Japan—Great Britain moved swiftly, in conjunction with the Soviet Union, to ensure allied possession of the Iranian oil fields, occupying the country in the process. Through London's control of the Kuwait Oil Company (KOC)—via British Petroleum—the British capped the newly discovered wells in the Burgan field to keep this resource out of German hands. Similarly, one could expect a prime objective in any major war of the future to be control of Middle Eastern oil at its source. Under such circumstances, monitoring of traffic through the Strait of Hormuz would become a lesser priority.

These waters would, however, be of crucial importance to nations—specifically those of the West—seeking to introduce military forces into the region to safeguard access to the oil. A glance at the map suggests that the best and most certain highway the United States and its allies could use to project power into the region would be a maritime one. Despite the incredible advances that have been made in air transport, the bulk of all military power being deployed globally—troops, equipment, and supplies—must still go by sea, and this is nowhere more true than with respect to Western movement into the northwest quadrant of the Indian Ocean. To understand the truth of this assertion, one need only look at the problems that would confront the United States should it undertake a major military move into the region.

In the early days of 1979, the White House decided that it had to demonstrate some form of support for Saudi Arabia in the wake of the shah's downfall in Iran. Washington elected to dispatch a small group of American fighter aircraft to the desert kingdom. We will avoid a debate over the nature and effectiveness of this particular show of force, centering as it did on the flight of a dozen unarmed F-15 interceptors from the United States to Saudi Arabia. The lesson to be learned from the experience, however, makes clear the difficulties encountered when attempting to move even minuscule military power by air halfway around the world. Denial of overflight and landing rights by nations enroute can make such an operation virtually impossible.

In an inexcusable foreign policy gaffe, the United States neglected to consult with the Spanish before announcing the projected flight. As it turned out, Madrid bluntly refused permission for the fighters to land at Torrejon, as planned, for refueling and rest. Consequently, the planes had to be refueled in the air throughout the entire distance, necessitating employment of a sizable portion of the nation's aerial tanker fleet—just to get a dozen fighter aircraft from the United States to Saudi Arabia. There would be a quantum increase in demand for aerial refueling to accompany any attempt to airlift, for example, 100,000 troops and their equipment to the region—even with the present inadequate C-5 fleet, the only U.S. transport aircraft with air-to-air refueling capabilities.

Without firm guarantees of ground support en route, the United States could not count on using even this limited method of augmenting its presently inadequate military strength in the northwest Indian Ocean/ Persian Gulf area. The only rational recourse available to Washington would be to reinforce its position by sea. In this instance, carriers operating in the Arabian Sea and the Gulf of Oman could blanket the Strait of Hormuz with air cover. Operations such as mine clearance and the transport of troops to the immediate vicinity of the all-important oil fields and facilities, however, would still require warships to transit the Strait. Thus, ensuring unfettered passage of these confined waters, although perhaps of secondary importance insofar as tanker traffic is concerned, would nonetheless assume critical dimensions under combat circumstances. To protect Saudi Arabian or Kuwaiti oil fields, for example, would necessitate the entry of sizable naval forces into the Persian Gulf itself. Should Iran fall to the Marxists or to Soviet occupation in any shooting war, Western naval forces— probably only those of the United States, France, and Great Britain—would be confronted with the prospects of fighting their way into the Gulf.

The foregoing threats would probably materialize during a shooting war involving local forces, or from a global war with intervention coming overland from the north, or in both instances. One must also consider threats from seaborne forces operating to the south of the Strait of Hormuz. These would appear to fall outside the scope of this inquiry, but closer examination suggests that they would constitute an integral part of the global problem that would surely confront Western defense planners in any wartime situation.

The first peril that comes to mind is that posed by the submarine. Used to blockade traffic attempting to exit the Persian Gulf, submarines would find water of adequate operating depth within easy range of the Strait itself. Moreover, the high temperatures and salinity found in this oceanic region render antisubmarine efforts difficult at best.

Moreover, in this age of nuclear-powered warships, attack submarines operating from the Soviet's Far Eastern bases—or perhaps from newly available ports such as Cam Ranh Bay in Vietnam—could remain on station in the Gulf of Oman for a period sufficient to make the effort worthwhile. Even the conventionally powered attack submarine—unable to perform usefully at great distances from a support base—could be comfortably staged out of friendly ports such as Aden in the People's Democratic Republic of Yemen (South Yemen) or from the naval base of Massawa in what is now a Marxist-ruled Ethiopia. Thus, the threat to shipping in the waters approaching the Strait of Hormuz could be quite real and exceedingly difficult to counter.

It would also be extremely unwise to overlook the possibility of action by Moscow's client states in the region. Although U.S. carrier airpower would make the waters on the Indian Ocean side of the Strait far too dangerous for operation of small missile boats from South Yemen or elsewhere, the situation on the Persian Gulf side of the Strait could be quite different. These dangerous craft, operating from Iraqi bases in the northern reaches of the Gulf, could pose serious threats to naval and merchant traffic inside the Strait of Hormuz.

Moreover, the foreign policy orientation of Iran in any such confrontation would be of crucial importance. Hovercraft and other light naval forces, hiding in ports along the Iranian coastline, could use the cover of darkness and the radar-masking effect of land and island masses to dart into the Strait and strike at shipping attempting to make the passage.

Another threat frequently cited is blockage of the Strait brought about by sinking one or more supertankers in these narrow waters. Although this would be a spectacular method of interrupting the flow of oil through the Strait, it cannot be considered realistic. As one Iranian naval officer put it, "the public's imagination appears to have overtaken common sense." Charts of the Strait of Hormuz reveal that depths well beyond the channels presently being used vary from 40 to 70 fathoms. A channel nearly four miles wide can be drawn on the chart with an average depth of 40 fathoms (240 feet). No supertanker in the world draws near to 100 feet. Even if one sank a dozen supertankers in these waters, the present inbound and outbound channels would still be usable. Moreover, there are miles of 30-fathom water adjacent to the four-mile-wide channel. The notion that the Strait could be blocked by sunken ships is a fallacy.

Mining, a threat already mentioned with respect to terrorist and local national actions, is even more probable in the event of major war. The Soviets possess a formidable mining capability, and the West, for its part, has a relatively poor mine countermeasure capacity. Inasmuch as Soviet access to the region's oil does not depend on transit of the Strait of Hormuz, Moscow would have very little to lose and a good deal to gain by seeding these waters with mines. Whether magnetic, acoustic, or pressure—fixed or mobile—mines present dangers so obvious and so powerful that they offer one certain means of shutting down traffic through the Strait for extended periods of time. Periodic reseeding could prevent use of these waters almost indefinitely. Furthermore, one should not forget the effects of a credible mining hoax.

The threats that can be presented to surface ships negotiating the waters of the Strait of Hormuz are many and varied. Whether or not one is discussing the lower end of the conflict spectrum or the possibility of full-scale warfare, it is obvious that those nations depending to a major degree on continued access to Middle Eastern oil must make adequate provision for ensuring safe passage through the Strait if they are to guarantee economic, hence political, survival until some viable alternative to petroleum is not only perfected, but brought on line.

This, of course, raises fundamental issues about the necessity for ensuring continuous access to Middle Eastern oil, especially in the event of a shooting war involving the two superpowers. The present Chief of Naval Operations, Admiral Thomas Hayward, has said that any NATO-Warsaw Pact war would necessarily be global in nature. One can easily argue that the converse is also true: Any war in which Western access to Middle Eastern oil is seriously threatened would require military action on the part of the NATO nations and that would most likely lead to a NATO-Warsaw Pact conflict. A war that carried the danger that the industrialized free world would be cut off from critical natural resources would almost certainly escalate to global dimensions. This would be especially true if the Soviet Union was clearly responsible. The question, then, is how the West can ensure access to Middle Eastern oil and assure itself of unfettered use of the waters that flow through the Strait of Hormuz.

MILITARY PROTECTION MEASURES

Promotion of political stability in and around the Persian Gulf region by nonmilitary means is obviously the first step that should be taken by the United States and its Western allies, but other preparations need to be made as well. It is altogether possible that armed force might be needed to preserve the West's vital interests in this part of the world.

It is not inconceivable that one or all of the various threats discussed will confront the Free World at one time or another. Heavily dependent on Middle Eastern oil, some of these nations—if they are to ensure themselves access to that oil—will have to examine those threats in detail and formulate plans to deal with them. This planning will include not only contingency plans for armed force, but ways to utilize this force in a coercive manner with a military presence. In view of the distances involved and the dearth of friendly bases in the Indian Ocean and Persian Gulf regions, such planning will pose operational and logistics difficulties almost as large as those in wartime.

Military options encompass a range of armed alternatives that can be employed before the commitment of U.S. or other Western military units. The first would be the enlistment of local armed forces. This concept, which became a cornerstone of American national security policy, originated during the tenure of President Richard M. Nixon.

Upon assuming office, Nixon decided that the United States should take a fresh look at how vital American interests were safeguarded around the world. Because of the extent of those interests, it seemed that the United States could accomplish the task only by maintaining prohibitively large armed forces and keeping sizable segments of these forces deployed to posts far from the continental United States. Thus, his administration fashioned what came to be known as the Nixon doctrine: The United States would draw back militarily from selected areas of the world and rely on local allies to make the primary contribution to self-defense and local security. The doctrine called for the following:

(1) more selective approach by the United States to its global role, particularly in the exercise of its military power;
(2) greater degree of burden-sharing by America's friends or allies in their own defense; and

(3) American help, primarily in the form of military assistance and sales, in the creation of independent power
centers to maintain local stability and help safeguard
American interests.

In the Persian Gulf, this doctrine was supplemented by
the twin pillar policy wherein the United States sought to
promote Saudi Arabian-Iranian cooperation in maintaining stability. This policy fit neatly into the plans of the
shah of Iran to acquire the armed muscle necessary to
protect the Iranian oil lifeline running the length of the
Gulf and to intervene where necessary to shore up the
royal and quasi-royal governments in the region. In
recent years the policy was strengthened further by the
decision of the Saudi Arabian government to embark on
a similar, if more modest, program to arm itself. Here the
United States played the major role in helping Riyadh
procure modern weaponry and training for its army,
navy, air force, and national guard, believing that close
cooperation between Iran and Saudi Arabia would ultimately evolve and U.S. security interests would be protected. The outcome of the rebellion in Oman seemed to
provide proof of the thesis.

This carefully fashioned edifice came tumbling down,
however, to be buried in the rubble of the Iranian revolution. By early 1979, it was clear that the foremost source
of local stability had suddenly become a threat to that
stability. Further, the shift of military primacy in the Gulf
to radical Iraq left the West in general and the United
States in particular with no foundation for the twin pillar
policy and with very shaky assets for support of the
Nixon Doctrine. In short, American policy toward the
Persian Gulf region was shattered along with the shah's
ambitions. That is not to say that local assistance in
containing threats to the Strait of Hormuz is wholly
unavailable, for it is.

Some nations in the region have forces—primarily naval and air—that are capable of dealing with those perils at the lower end of the threat spectrum (that is, piracy and terrorism). First, there is Iranian power, although we are not sure at this time whether it is an asset or a threat. Next, there is the small sea wing of the U.A.E. defense force. Beyond that is the naval strength of Saudi Arabia. For the present, the Royal Saudi Naval Forces exist in name only, and it will probably be several years before they will have the ability to assume some of the responsibility for security of Gulf waters, especially those of the Strait.

The naval forces of Oman are still small; their hands are full protecting mere portions, let alone the whole, of the Sultanate's long coastline. Nevertheless, Sultan Qaboos boasts one significant asset that can be put to excellent use: the Musandam peninsula. As already noted in the threat assessment, this spit of sand could be used as a place from which to attack shipping or help protect it.

In reviewing the threats posed by pirates and terrorists, it seems clear that terrorists in dhows or other small craft could be countered by the modest forces presently in the area and, to some extent, by land forces based on the Musandam peninsula. Moreover, equipping nations on the Arabian side of the Gulf with modern mine-sweeping and hunting capabilities would also serve that purpose.

Given the comparatively greater dependence of Western European nations and Japan on the flow of oil through the Strait of Hormuz, their acceptance of responsibility for defense of the oil route should be raised. To date, it is clear that none of these nations— with the exception of France and Great Britain—who might act unilaterally—has evinced any willingness to address the problem.

The North Atlantic Alliance has repeatedly refused to consider any alteration to the defensive frontiers of NATO, particularly its maritime boundaries. Today, as has been the case for more than three decades, the Tropic of Cancer marks the southern boundary for those waters falling under the protection of the alliance. Thus, the member states continue their practice of taking advantage of the navies of major maritime powers. In years past this may have been an acceptable, if admittedly cynical, approach to their respective security problems, but it no longer can be justified. The steady decline in the strength of the United States and Royal Navies in recent years simply means that the maritime prowess necessary to meet the challenges on the oceans beyond NATO's boundaries—although continuing to safeguard the Atlantic approaches to Western Europe and the waters of the Mediterranean—is no longer available.

What should be done about it? The most forthright answer is that every member of the alliance should devote money, men, and material—land, sea, and air—to the task of preserving Western access to the oil fields of the Middle East. Any realisitic observer of international, especially alliance, affairs, however, can only conclude that this is not going to happen. Therefore, there must be some other solution.

Only slightly less improbable than the foregoing resolution is the suggestion that Great Britain and France—in conjunction with the United States—act to guarantee the flow of oil from the Middle East to NATO countries. It is altogether likely that Great Britain would shrink from such an exercise, just as it has from the simple act of boycotting the Olympic games in Moscow, and that France, the maverick of the Western alliance, would be far more likely to take independent action. If one accepts this assessment, still other alternatives must then be sought.

If NATO were to play a role in this area, the most likely would be for it to assume greater responsibility for the ground and air defense of the continent against the threat of Warsaw Pact aggression. It might then also assume responsibility for naval defense of the reenforcement and resupply lines from the United States and Canada to Western Europe. All of this would, of course, require substantial increases in defense expenditures. In light of NATO's past record of meeting defense needs — a modest record, given the huge American commitment — this outlook, although better than the outlook for concerted action for intervention in the Middle East, is something less than realistic.

Perhaps a naval effort alone is the only feasible solution. If the European nations were to undertake building programs for the construction of open-ocean escorts and maritime patrol aircraft to combat the Soviet submarine menace, and long-range, intercept aircraft to defend against the antishipping threat posed by the Soviet Backfire bomber, significant advances toward defense of the vital oil line from the Persian Gulf could be achieved. European assumption of such naval responsibilities in the North Atlantic would release powerful American naval units for employment in the Indian Ocean region.

A similar case can be made for the U.S. naval deployments in the Mediterranean Sea. In the days before the advent of the long-range bomber equipped with precision-guided, air-to-surface missiles, the presence of two U.S. attack aircraft carrier battle groups in that sea could be justified. This is no longer the case. Careful observers of the naval scene are convinced that the first U.S. naval move at the outbreak of a European war would be to retire at least to the western Mediterranean to ensure survival in the face of the Soviet airborne threat. Would it not be better, then, that these ships be removed from the Mediterranean now for use in other, more distant areas vital to NATO, with their present responsibilities being assumed by air and sea forces of NATO's Mediterranean members? One would think so.

III. A Permanent U.S. Naval Presence in the Indian Ocean

Thomas H. Moorer and Alvin J. Cottrell

Threats to the interests of the United States and its allies in the Persian Gulf-Strait of Hormuz region point to the need for U.S. countermeasures to arrest the erosion of political stability. This threat was dramatically heightened by the swift political changes that occurred in Iran after the fall of the Iranian monarchy in early 1979. This development finally forced the U.S. government to recognize that a permanent, sizable U.S. naval presence

NOTE: Grateful acknowledgment is extended to the U.S. Strategic Institute for permission to reprint this chapter, which appeared as an article entitled "The Search for U.S. Bases in the Indian Ocean: A Last Chance" in the Spring 1980 issue of *Strategic Review* (Vol. VIII, No. 2).

would be required if there were to be any chance of reversing the trends running against the United States in that vital area.

Since February 1979, the United States has been faced with the progressive instability in the northern rim of the Middle East—from Turkey to Iran, Afghanistan, and Pakistan. In the Eisenhower-Dulles era, the strategic Northern Tier was designed to block the Soviet Union's southward expansion; it now lies in shambles. And the reverberations are threatening the fragile political structures of the Arabian Peninsula, putting at risk the sources of vital Western oil supplies.

BATTERED ASSUMPTIONS

It is painfully evident that the United States is reaping today in this crescent of crisis the penalty for three decades of strategic neglect. What deepens the irony is that this neglect was not so much the product of global circumstance, but rather the result of willful strategy. In the postwar period, the United States made major investments in military forces and strategic infrastructure in the North Atlantic region and the Pacific Basin. The vast region between those two areas of massive U.S. power projection was left essentially free of any means for forward deployment, let alone of a U.S. military presence other than a token Middle East fleet of three antiquated naval vessels.

Until the late 1960s, a convenient justification for this strategic neglect was that the region was still patrolled (if by no means controlled) by the residual elements of British imperial power. But even this pretext fell away in 1968, when Great Britain announced a total withdrawal of its remaining military forces east of Suez—a decision that was almost immediately followed by the first deployments of what is now a substantial Soviet naval and air presence. These danger signals—sharpened by Soviet and Cuban activity in Africa and the Middle East, as well as by the repercussions of the 1973 Arab oil embargo—prompted intensified discussion in the United States about policies in the area, but little in the way of concrete measures. Indeed, one of the first actions by the Carter administration in 1977 was to initiate negotiations with the Soviet Union leading toward a demilitarization of the Indian Ocean. That effort was abandoned (or suspended) only after massive Soviet and Cuban intervention in the Horn of Africa underscored its absurdity.

In retrospect, America's strategic neglect of the Indian Ocean-Persian Gulf region was the product not so much of considerations of strategy or resource constraints but of three widespread assumptions within the U.S. policy community—assumptions that flourished in the 1960s and survived the danger signals of the past decade.

The first assumption was that there was no meaningful relationship between visible U.S. military power and regional political stability. The assumption, which gained strength in the context of the debates over the Vietnam conflict, was that not only does showing the flag fail to win friends and influence people in remote regions, but also that it is counterproductive—evoking memories of gunboat diplomacy. It is ironic that this assumption was applied to a region that historically has been at the mercy of external power, particularly naval power, and where respect for power has traditionally swayed regional attitudes and politics more profoundly than elsewhere on the globe.

A second and corollary assumption was related to the Soviet military buildup in the Indian Ocean. Those in the U.S. foreign policy community who opposed any new projection of U.S. power into the region naturally discounted both the intentions behind and the implications of expanding Soviet military presence. They argued, first, that Moscow's efforts in the area were not aimed at aggrandizement, but rather represented a preemptive strategy vis-à-vis a feared encirclement of the Soviet Union by China. But the major contention was that, irrespective of the motives behind Soviet strategy, Moscow would soon learn the painful truth: The display of military muscle would not buy the Kremlin any political advantages in the region. Indeed, the Soviets would find themselves hopelessly caught in the brambles of local nationalism, at heavy cost to Soviet treasure and prestige.

A third assumption was perhaps the crucial one: U.S. and Western economic stakes in the region did not need military protection because they would survive the tremors caused by change. The argument supporting this assumption is in three parts: (1) sociopolitical change in such anachronistic places as Iran, Saudi Arabia, and the shaikhdoms of the Gulf is not only inevitable, but desirable; (2) the United States should ally itself with the forces of change; and (3) no new regime, no matter how revolutionary, would deliberately harm itself by threatening Western economic interests, denying itself the needed national revenues. The argument, in short, was that the dictates of economic advantage would inevitably triumph over ideological fervor and revolutionary turmoil.

All of these assumptions have been undermined by the succession of events beginning with the Arab oil boycott of 1973-1974 and climaxing in the convulsions in Iran and the Soviet invasion of Afghanistan. The United States is now in the predicament of having to confront a whole range of contingencies in the Persian Gulf-Indian Ocean region that could call for the application of military power—without the effective support for projecting such power.

IS TIME RUNNING OUT?

In an effort to solve this predicament, the United States is now engaged in a quest for the means to sustain a military role in the region. The efforts include the current deployment of U.S. naval vessels and Marine components to the area, longer-range plans for the creation of a Rapid Deployment Force, and a much-publicized search for needed air and naval facilities to support meaningful and flexible U.S. military capabilities in the future.

The nagging question that hovers over these efforts—which are being conducted in an atmosphere of near frenzy—is whether they are not already too late. The question is a result of the rapid tide of events in the region, as well as of the delicate interaction of factors that go into the acquisition of military facilities abroad or rights of access to such facilities.

As far as timing is concerned, the current U.S. naval deployment in the region already underscores the penalties of past U.S. procrastination. In the spring of 1980 the United States had done on a relatively massive scale what it chose not to do on even a relatively modest basis as recently as a year and a half before: It had dispatched two carriers and their supporting surface capabilities to the northwestern Indian Ocean region, principally to the Arabian Sea adjacent to the Persian Gulf-South Asian littoral. This large-scale escalation of the U.S. naval presence in the Indian Ocean was made necessary by the failure to stage a more measured buildup of U.S. power in the years following Great Britain's withdrawal from the region—particularly after 1973, when the expansion of Soviet power, the deterioration of regional stability, and the threats to vital U.S. interests were obvious.

In international crisis management, as in local law enforcement, anticipatory, preventive measures are more cost-effective than a hurried, haphazard assembling of reactive forces once a crisis is raging and threatening to spread out of control. And there is little question that the current U.S. naval deployment in the Indian Ocean is both reactive and haphazard. The naval force has been drawn essentially from carrier forces of the U.S. Seventh Fleet in the Pacific, where they have exercised the traditional and increasingly significant task of supporting political stability in East Asia. These forces cannot be spared very long without causing China, Japan, the Philippines, and other nations to question their own future orientation if there should be even more tenuous links to U.S. military power.

At some point, therefore, the U.S. vessels currently in the Indian Ocean will have to return to Pacific waters. Looking to the future and to the broader aggregation of naval and air power and supporting facilities on land that the United States will have to put together in the Indian Ocean, we may not need as large a force as 25 vessels. Something along the lines of the Sixth Fleet Task Force 60.2, which operates in the Mediterranean with one carrier and nine other vessels, may well prove adequate to the mission. In the meantime the current naval presence is necessary to demonstrate U.S. resolve, to effect a shift in the geopolitical momentum in the region, and to serve as a backdrop for U.S. efforts to establish an infrastructure of supporting bases and facilities. Furthermore, it is important for regional perceptions that a formal fleet designation be given to whatever U.S. naval presence is retained in the region.

The intangible but undeniable phenomenon of geopolitical momentum brings us to the problem of U.S. base acquisition and access to facilities and airspace in the region. The United States should have learned in three postwar decades that, even under the most promising circumstances, this problem is a delicate one. No sovereign nation easily accepts the military presence—or even the tokens of such presence—of another nation on its own territory. Against any potential benefits derived by the host country from the granting of base and access rights there is usually an array of tangible risks: (1) no matter how qualified the arrangement is by contractual language, it represents some impingement on a nation's sovereignty; (2) it renders the host country a more conspicuous military (and political) target; (3) the influx of foreign personnel invariably leads to local frictions; (4) for all of the above reasons, foreign bases or access rights can become the focal point for domestic political opposition and revolutionary movements.

Of all the factors that go into the decision by any given country to grant such rights, the dominant factor is the nation's perception of its own security. This perception, in turn, arises not simply from the fear of aggression, but also from a positive belief in the ability and willingness of the guest power to help against aggression and to give that measure of extra protection against the heightened risks incurred by the base privileges themselves. The host country, in short, looks for what may be called "preferred risk insurance."

For 15 years after the end of World War II, the United States encountered no great obstacles in obtaining overseas base rights and military access privileges. Within the past decade, the global logistic structure of the United States, the underpinning of its strategic mobility, has crumbled dangerously, precisely because of shifts in world power and the lessening credibility of the United States as a guarantor of local security.

This means that in the Indian Ocean-Persian Gulf region, where the United States is seeking not to retain old military footholds but to create new ones, it faces an uphill battle. The political terrain is not altogether unfavorable, however, as a result of new fears in the region that have been spawned by revolutionary turmoil and

Soviet expansion. But time seems limited. The situation calls for speed and adroitness—the kind of adroitness that the United States has not shown in its dealings with Pakistan.

Much of the media's reporting on the question of U.S. basing rights in the Persian Gulf-South Asian area stresses that many of the regional states say they do not want U.S. bases. The word "bases" is the key word. If any leader in the region is asked if he is willing to provide the United States with a "base," the answer will be no. That is why officials in Kenya, Oman, and Pakistan emphasize that they are not prepared to give the United States bases, but instead are discussing the possibility of increased access to local facilities, such as ports and airfields. This is an important distinction, one that conforms to modern political imperatives.

INITIAL STEPS: DIEGO GARCIA, KENYA, SOMALIA

The U.S. Navy is planning for the further development of the island of Diego Garcia in the Chagos Archipelago as a basing facility for a U.S. task force or fleet in the Indian Ocean. This program is scheduled to cost about $170 million over a four-year period beginning in FY 1981, with an initial cost of $78 million. In 1976, some influential liberal members of the U.S. Senate had strongly opposed construction of the Diego Garcia facility. Senator John Culver proposed an amendment to the military appropriations bill that would have halted the use of authorized funds for the development of Diego Garcia until the president reported to the Congress the administration's efforts to negotiate with the Soviets on demilitarization and naval arms limitations in the Indian Ocean.

The Culver amendment was turned down at that time by the Ford administration largely on the grounds that the negotiations on such matters were not in the U.S. interest while the Soviet Union and its Cuban surrogates were actively engaged in support of revolution in Africa, especially in Angola. As has been noted, the Carter administration subsequently initiated such negotiations.

Diego Garcia has become the only stable U.S. facility in the Indian Ocean because it is owned by Great Britain, is sparsely inhabited, and is thus relatively immune to political disturbances. However, although Diego Garcia, more than 2000 miles from the Persian Gulf, represents an excellent site for supporting deployments into the area, it cannot substitute for facilities closer to the potential theater.

In Kenya the United States gained access rights for wider use of facilities. U.S. naval forces, especially carrier forces, have been calling at the Kenyan port of Mombasa for years. The value of the port to U.S. naval deployments has risen ever since the United States lost access to the French base at Diego-Suarez on the northern tip of Madagascar and to the equally important port facility at Maputo (formerly Lourenco Marques) in Mozambique. Yet Kenya is some 2500 miles from the Strait of Hormuz—about the same distance as Diego Garcia—and could serve only as a supporting area for deployments to the Arabian Peninsula-Persian Gulf littoral. Kenya's airport could also be used for supporting U.S. air operations in the northwestern quadrant of the Indian Ocean.

The United States has successfully negotiated access to facilities in Somalia, particularly to the former Soviet naval base at Berbera and the airstrip behind the base, which is 14,700 feet long and provides a convenient platform for aerial surveillance of the northern part of the Cape sea route. Berbera also has the advantage of being more than 1000 miles closer to the Strait of Hormuz than is Diego Garcia.

There would be a broader political advantage to a U.S. military presence at Berbera: the reassurance that this presence would convey to Saudi Arabia, which is deeply apprehensive of the Soviet-Cuban presence in Ethiopia on the Horn of Africa and in South Yemen. The question of possible U.S. access to Saudi Arabia itself will be discussed below. Meanwhile, it is worth noting that the failure by the United States to deploy a carrier task force to the region during the Somalia-Ethiopia War of 1977, when the Soviet Union and Cuba were massively and successfully supporting Ethiopia, prompted the first strong Saudi misgivings about the credibility of the United States as a factor in the regional power equation.

Some of these political losses in Riyadh could be recouped through a U.S. presence on Somalian soil, directly across the Gulf of Aden from Soviet-dominated South Yemen and by the U.S. presence at the Egyptian facility at Ras Banas on the Red Sea. Yet, objections have already arisen in the U.S. administration about providing even low-level military assistance to Somalia as a quid pro quo for the use of the strategically important facilities in Berbera. The argument is that such U.S. weapons in Somalia hands, if used in the fighting in the Ogaden, could somehow embroil the United States in a direct confrontation with the Soviet Union. It is this kind of overcautiousness that has played a major role in America's global retreat and that could abort the search for a new global posture before it has begun.

THE POTENTIAL IN OMAN

Oman is a key state that has been cautiously favorable to U.S. basing rights. It exercises sovereignty over the tip of the Musandam peninsula, only 21 miles from the

Iranian shore. The remainder of Oman's territory, which is not contiguous with this small spit of land, is south of Hormuz and offers one of the most important strategic footholds on the Arabian peninsula.

The United States already has enjoyed relatively free access to the airfield on Masirah, an Omani island about seven miles wide and 25 miles long, located about 500 miles south of the Musandam peninsula in the Gulf of Oman. Formerly a Royal Air Force base, Masirah also served as a potential British staging base for military operations in the Gulf region. The base is being improved for the possible staging of U.S. forces in the region.

Experts familiar with Masirah's facilities have estimated that the British could have staged 25,000 forces through the island fairly rapidly to meet their regional commitments. Since the departure of the British about two years ago, Sultan Qaboos has granted the United States access to the former British base, and the United States reportedly intends to use it for surveillance of the northwest quadrant of the Indian Ocean. The island of Masirah itself could also be used as a staging base: it offers political as well as security advantages. Because the island is sparsely inhabited, there is less risk of the kinds of local friction so often encountered around mainland facilities. By that same token, Masirah is also less vulnerable to the standard guerrilla and terrorist incursions that are more difficult to cope with on the mainland.

More generally, Oman, including Masirah Island, is well situated for the prepositioning of supplies and spare parts for U.S. forces in the region. Such prepositioning is not only militarily vital, but also serves the all-important political and psychological function of signaling in a tangible form a durable U.S. military commitment. If there are direct U.S. stakes to be defended, then the assurance to the host country becomes commensurately more persuasive.

In deference to regional political sensitivities, Oman has announced that it does not wish U.S. combat forces on its soil but that the United States will have to provide for the protection of whatever facilities might be introduced. Oman's stance presents a dilemma. Conceivably, the problem of safeguarding facilities on Masirah might be solved through the presence of the kind of reinforced Marine battalion that was dispatched to the Persian Gulf in February 1980.

A clear quid pro quo for the use of facilities in Oman would be the commitment of U.S. military support to the Sultan in the event of a new flare-up of the rebellion in the Dhofar province. A Marine force of the strength mentioned above would suffice for this task. In 1974, when the last rebellion was largely put down, Iranian troops consisting of at most 3500 relatively untrained soldiers actually outnumbered the rebels. In any event, the United States must be prepared to assist the sultan and his British advisers (who number about 500) if the rebellion is rekindled from South Yemen with Cuban and Soviet support. A U.S. military presence in or near Oman might do much to deter a revival of the Dhofar insurgency.

The United States is also seeking greater use of the Omani ports at Muscat and Salalah. Either port could add substantially to the U.S. infrastructure for forward deployment to the Persian Gulf-Gulf of Oman region. Muscat is only about 400 miles from the Hormuz narrows and is thus an excellent location for supporting a variety of operations in the Arabian Peninsula. Muscat is also served by a first-class airport, which could be used for the prepositioning of heavy equipment and supplies and for aircraft refueling operations.

The importance of Oman as a potential staging area for U.S. forward deployments in the region is underscored by the apparently limited chance of any meaningful U.S. peacetime access to Saudi Arabia. Indeed, the Saudi reluctance to allow U.S. bases on its soil speaks all too eloquently for the desert kingdom's dwindling faith in its links with the United States. Perhaps the tangible token of a regional U.S. posture will serve to strengthen that faith, and with it will come greater Saudi willingness to engage in open military cooperation. In the meantime, the U.S. administration apparently is seeking the right to preposition some supplies in Saudi Arabia and is encouraging the Saudis to develop airfield facilities to accomodate U.S. aircraft if they should be needed.

POSSIBLE FACILITIES IN PAKISTAN

The quest by the United States for a regional basing structure is a delicate undertaking—one that has to be conducted within the broader context of U.S. security policies in the area, with emphasis upon military assistance programs. The case of Pakistan illustrates that the U.S. administration still fails to grasp this fact.

We have mentioned the attractions of the Omani island of Masirah and talked of the possibility of building a naval facility on the island, although the cost of such a project would be extremely high. There are other excellent potential naval facilities in the Gulf of Oman area that are much better suited topographically and that could be developed at relatively lower cost. One such site is on former Omani territory across the Arabian Sea from Oman: the port at the fishing village of Gwadar in the Pakistani province of Baluchistan.

In 1973-1974 the government of the late Prime Minister Ali Bhutto offered this facility to the United States for development in return for a lifting of the U.S. arms embargo to Pakistan, but the offer was not accepted by the United States. Gwadar is an ideal spot, located just where the Gulf of Oman becomes the Arabian Sea, and it offers to the United States the potential for a convenient facility outside the Hormuz-Gulf of Oman narrows that would be more secure than facilities inside the Strait itself.

Gwadar is in a remote part of Pakistan, where Baluchi tribesmen are seeking greater autonomy from Islamabad. The Soviets have obvious designs on this area in their drive for direct access to the Indian Ocean. Their presence in Afghanistan leaves them now only 350 miles from Hormuz and the Arabian Sea, and an independent Baluchistan under Moscow's control would provide them with that corridor of access. Indeed, there have already been unconfirmed reports from Turkish intelligence sources that Soviet forces are giving military training to Baluchi tribesmen in southern Afghanistan.

At relatively low cost, Gwadar could be made into an anchorage. The major components needed would be a crane for lifting supplies, fuel tanks, and a barge to bring fuel to the ships if they could not move alongside. A U.S. naval facility in this area could also deter the Soviet drive southward. The history of the last three decades has amply demonstrated that wherever the United States has stationed a permanent military presence—in Europe or in Korea—Soviet strategy has become substantially more circumspect. U.S. policymakers, who are forever expressing concern about the dangers of being drawn into a direct confrontation with the Soviet Union, have yet to appreciate that the Soviets tend to shy away from such confrontations as well.

The United States could benefit from access to the large Pakistani air base at Peshawar—where the U-2 flights refueled in the early 1960s—not as an American base, but as a combined U.S.-Pakistani facility to maintain surveillance over Soviet activities in the Northwest Frontier Province area and, if necessary, counter those activities. Yet, in order to be able to use facilities in Pakistan as they were used in the early 1960s, the United States must first provide Pakistan with relatively long-term military assistance to rebuild its military forces, which have been deteriorating badly since the 1971 war with India.

Pakistan, while jolted by the Soviet move into Afghanistan, has been worried about the durability of newly expressed U.S. concern over the threat to South Asia. A principal Pakistani objection to a proposed U.S. $400 million arms package by the Carter administration was the suggestion that the agreement be of only two years' duration. As high-ranking Pakistani officials have pointed out to the authors, two years is far too short a time to build up the Pakistani forces adequately, and they are fearful that the United States would back off from continuing this assistance after two years, leaving Pakistan once again to bear the brunt of Soviet displeasure for its ties with the United States. The Pakistanis vividly remember their predicament in this respect following the disclosure that the Pakistani air base at Peshawar was used as a refueling and takeoff point for the U.S. U-2 flights.

Pakistan's position is quite understandable; it is unwilling to accept aid that promises to be so limited in duration and quantity as to be inadequate in light of threats to the region, and that at the same time would expose the country to attacks from Moscow and elements in the Arab world (such as Libya). The amount of aid requested—about $1.5 billion—is necessary to offset such concerns.

U.S. support of and confidence in Pakistan can be demonstrated only by sales of the more sophisticated military equipment that the Pakistanis have wanted since 1965 over the inevitable objections of the government of India. The Indian government's strictures against the transfer to Pakistan of such weapons systems as the A-7 ground-attack aircraft make little sense, given India's overwhelming superiority over Pakistan in both quantity and quality of aircraft. The quantitative superiority stands at least six to one, and India can widen this gap by manufacturing MIGs in Indian factories under a licensing agreement with the Soviet Union. The failure by the United States to sell 25 to 30 of the A-7 aircraft to Pakistan also becomes a sensitive political issue because it is seen as a lack of trust on our part. Pakistan has need of more advanced aircraft to defend against armored forces crossing into Pakistani territory or even a possible Soviet drive to fashion a corridor through Baluchistan to the Arabian Sea. The United States cannot continue to permit India to exercise a veto power over U.S. arms policies to Pakistan.

Other facilities in Pakistan potentially of value to the United States are the Karachi airfield and seaport, which U.S. forces used in the MIDLINK maneuvers under the CENTO Treaty when Pakistan was still a member. Such arrangements would include the right to deploy several squadrons of replacement aircraft there for U.S. carriers and the right to preposition naval fuel, spare parts, and other supplies.

The Karachi facilities, both the seaport and the airport, could provide excellent locations for the transfer of heavy spare parts for ships. If acceptable to the Pakistanis, the Karachi port could serve as an anchorage for a tender to repair surface ships (at present the U.S. surface tender *Dixie* is based in Diego Garcia). The Karachi airport would also be well situated for emergency landings—if carrier flights had to be aborted—as well as a base for refueling aircraft to support carrier and other aircraft operations in the area. The question of facilities in Pakistan should be pursued by the Reagan administration.

NO MARGIN FOR ERROR

One can only hope that the much-publicized search for U.S. facilities in the Indian Ocean-Persian Gulf region will be successful and that those facilities will serve to enhance the ability of the United States to counter Soviet expansion and other threats to vital Western economic and strategic stakes in the area. The task would have been substantially easier had the appropriate importance been attached to the Indian Ocean as recently as 1973. At least the Ford administration, against strong congressional opposition, forced through the development of U.S. facilities in Diego Garcia, which can now be used as the central backup base for a forward projection of force to the littoral of the Horn of Africa-Arabian Sea region.

No area is more critical to the economic and political survival of the United States and its Western allies than the Arabian Peninsula. Yet, this area is far from the United States—over 20 ship days or 11,000 miles from either coast of the United States. Thus, at a time when the strength of the U.S. Navy has been cut from 1000 ships to less than 500 over the past decades, we must have forward facilities to support and sustain our limited number of platforms.

Efforts to establish a permanent, large-scale U.S. military presence in the Indian Ocean, and especially its northwestern quadrant, were thwarted by opposition in the past by both Congress and the Carter administration until it was jolted by the present crisis.

There is still a chance to reestablish the military credibility of the United States in this all-important sector of the Indian Ocean. This is clearly the last chance.

The deterioration of the U.S. posture in this area has been allowed to progress to the point where it would be difficult to reverse. Geopolitical time is growing extremely short. Even if relative calm should return to the Persian Gulf-South Asia region—which seems likely as the Soviets stabilize their position in Afghanistan—the United States must nevertheless continue to pursue its buildup in the area. The crisis will remain irrespective of

NOTES

1. According to Samuel Eliot Morison (1978), the price of cloves went from two ducats to ten ducats per hundredweight over a five-year period in the 1530s. Along with spices, trade with the East also included Chinese and Persian silks, Indian cotton, Chinese emeralds, and rubies and sapphires from India, Burma, and Ceylon.

2. Alfred Thayer Mahan (1840-1914), America's great naval strategist, is considered one of the most influential military theorists of all time. A United States naval officer and historian, Mahan lectured on the history of naval warfare and the theories of naval power at the Naval War College in Newport, Rhode Island.

In his most significant works, *The Influence of Sea Power in History, 1660-1783* (published in 1890), and *The Influence of Sea Power on the French Revolution and Empire* (1892),

Mahan maintained that control of the seas led to success in international politics.

3.   In addition to agreed extensions of territorial seas and EEZs, there are a number of disturbing unilateral claims by littoral states that have potentially destabilizing effects in some areas. These include security zones such as that imposed by North Korea, archipelago claims such as those made by Indonesia, pollution zones, and sector claims for the Arctic such as those made by Canada and the USSR.

4.   The analogy with present-day shipborne cruise missiles is discussed in detail in an excellent article by Michael Vlahos, "A Crack in the Shield: The Capital Ship Under Attack," in *The Journal of Strategic Studies,* May 1979.

REFERENCES

BROWN, H. (1902) The Venetian Republic. London: Bedford
Street Press.

HOLT, P.B., A. LAMBTON, and B. LEWIS [eds.] (1970)
Cambridge History of Islam. Volume 1A. Cambridge: At
the University Press.

MACPHERSON, A. (1812) European Commerce with India.
London: Longman Hurst et al.

MORISON, S.E. (1978) The Great Explorers: The European
Discovery of America. New York: Oxford University Press.

PARRY, F.H. (1967) in E.E. Rich and C.H. Wilson (eds.) The
Cambridge Economic History of Europe. Volume 1V.
Cambridge: At the University Press.

RICHARDSON, E.L. (1979) Speech 14 July at Bath, Maine.

BIBLIOGRAPHY

ADIE, W.A.C. (1975) Oil, Politics and Seapower: The Indian Ocean Vortex. New York: Crane, Russak & Co.

AMIRIE, ABBAS [ed.] (1975) The Persian Gulf and Indian Ocean in International Politics. Tehran: Institute for international Political and Economic Studies.

ANTHONY, JOHN DUKE (1975) Arab States of the Lower Gulf: People, Politics, Petroleum. Washington, DC: The Middle East Institute.

Central Intelligence Agency (1976) Indian Ocean Atlas. Washington, DC: Government Printing Office.

CHUBIN, SHAHRAM (1976) "Naval competition and security in South-West Asia," in Power at Sea III: Competition and Conflict. Adelphi Paper No. 124. London: International Institute for Strategic Studies.

Collected Papers of the Study Conference on the Indian Ocean in International Politics (1973). Southampton, England: University of Southampton.

COTTRELL, ALVIN J. and FRANK BRAY (1978) Military Forces in the Persian Gulf. Washington Paper No. 60. Beverly Hills, CA: Sage.

COTTRELL, ALVIN J. and R.M. BURRELL [eds.] (1974) The Indian Ocean: Its Political, Economic, and Military Importance. New York: Praeger.

COTTRELL, ALVIN J. and JAMES E. DOUGHERTY (1977) Iran's Quest for Security: U.S. Arms Transfers and the Nuclear Option. Cambridge: Institute for Foreign Policy Analysis.

COTTRELL, ALVIN J. and WALTER F. HAHN (1978) Naval Race or Arms Control in the Indian Ocean. New York: National Strategy Information Center.

———(1976) Soviet Shadow over Africa. Florida: Center for Advanced International Studies, University of Miami.

DONALDSON, ROBERT H. (1974) Soviet Policy Toward India: Ideology and Strategy. Cambridge: Harvard University Press.

FAIRHALL, DAVID (1971) Russian Sea Power. Boston: Gambit.

FIENNES, RANULPH (1975) Where Soldiers Fear To Tread. (This book concerns the insurrection in Oman.) London: Hoddr and Stoughton.

HALLIDAY, FRED (1974) Arabia Without Sultans. Harmondsworth, England: Penguin.

HAWLEY, DONALD (1977) Oman and Its Renaissance. London: Stacey International.

———(1970) The Trucial States. London: George Allen & Unwin.

HAYES, JAMES H. (1974) Indian Ocean Geopolitics. Rand Report No. P-5325. Santa Monica, CA: Rand.

HOLLICK, ANN L. and ROBERT OSGOOD (1974) New Era of Ocean Politics. Baltimore: Johns Hopkins University Press.

JUKES, GEOFFREY (1972) The Indian Ocean in Soviet Naval Policy. Adelphi Paper No. 87. London: International Institute for Strategic Studies.

KHADDURI, MAJID (1978) Socialist Iraq: A Study in Iraq Politics Since 1968. Washington, DC: The Middle East Institute.

LENCZOWSKI, GEORGE (1978) Iran under the Pahlavis. Stanford: Hoover Institution Press.

LONG, DAVID E. (1978) The Persian Gulf. Boulder, CO: Westview Press.

McEWAN, C.B. (1979) Lifeline or Strategic Backwater: The Military Significance of the Cape Sea Routes. Capetown, South Africa: Cape and Transvaal Printers.

McGRUTHER, KENNETH R. (1978) The Evolving Soviet Navy. Newport, RI: Naval War College.

McGUIRE, MICHAEL (1975) Soviet Naval Policy. New York: Praeger.

———[ed.] (1973) Soviet Naval Developments: Capabilities and Context. New York: Praeger.

MALONE, JOSEPH (1973) The Arab Lands of Western Asia. Englewood Cliffs, NJ: Prentice-Hall.

MILLAR, T.B. (1970) Soviet Policies in the Indian Ocean Area. Canberra: Australian National University Press.

———(1969) The Indian and Pacific Oceans. Some Strategic Considerations. Adelphi Paper No. 57. London: International Institute for Strategic Studies.

NATHAN, JAMES A. and JAMES K. OLIVER (1979) The Future of the United Sea Power. Bloomington: Indiana University Press.

NITZE, PAUL et al. (1979) Securing the Seas: The Soviet Naval Challenge and Western Options. Washington, DC: The Atlantic Council.

NYROP, R.F. et al. (1977a) Area Handbook for Saudi Arabia. Washington, DC: Government Printing Office.

———(1977b) Area Handbook for the Persian Gulf States. Washington, DC: Government Printing Office.

PANIKKAR, K.M. (1957) India and the Indian Ocean. An Essay on the Influence of Sea Power on Indian History. London: George Allen & Unwin.

POULOSE, T.T. (1974) Indian Ocean Power Rivalry. New Delhi: Young Asia Publications.

RAMAZANI, ROUHOLLAH K. (1979) The Persian Gulf and the Strait of Hormuz. The Netherlands: Sythoff and Noordhoff.

———(1975) Iran's Foreign Policy, 1941-1973: A Study of Foreign Policy in Modernizing Nations. Charlottesville: University of Virginia.

SMITH, H.H. et al. (1971) Area Handbook for Iran. Washington, DC: Government Printing Office.

———(1969) Area Handbook for Iraq. Washington, DC: Government Printing Office.

SPAIN, JAMES W. (1972) The Way of the Pathans. Karachi: Oxford University Press.

STODDARD, THEODORE et al. (1971) Area Handbook for Indian Ocean Territories. Washington, DC: Government Printing Office.

SZYLIOWICZ, JOSEPH S. and BARD E. O'NEILL [eds.] (1975) The Energy Crisis and U.S. Foreign Policy. New York: Praeger.

THOMSON, GEORGE C. (1970) Problems of Strategy in the Pacific and Indian Oceans. New York: National Strategy Information Center.

TOUSSAINT, AUGUSTE (1966) History of the Indian Ocean. Chicago: University of Chicago Press.

TOWNSEND, JOHN (1977) Oman: The Making of a Modern State. London: Helm.

UDOVITCH, A.L. [ed.] (1976) The Middle East: Oil Conflict & Hope. Lexington, MA: D.C. Heath.

VALI, FERENC (1976) Politics of the Indian Ocean Region. New York: Free Press.

INDEX

ABOUT THE AUTHORS

Alvin J. Cottrell, Executive Director for Maritime Policy Studies of Georgetown University's Center for Strategic and International Studies (CSIS), received his Ph.D. from the University of Pennsylvania and attended the National War College, where he was professor of foreign affairs. He has made numerous visits to the Mediterranean, Middle East, and Indian Ocean regions and has met with key leaders from these areas. Dr. Cottrell authored four *Washington Papers;* his other publications include *The Indian Ocean: Its Political, Military, and Economic Importance* (1972), *Soviet Shadow Over Africa* (1976), *Indian Ocean Naval Limitations* (1976), and *The Persian Gulf States* (1980).

Rear Admiral Robert J. Hanks, USN (Ret.) was Director, Strategic Plans, Policy, Nuclear Systems and National Security

Council Affairs Division, Office of the Chief of Naval Operations, at the time of his retirement in 1977. Currently he is a consultant on U.S. maritime policy to CSIS and also consultant to the Institute for Foreign Policy Analysis. His earlier assignments include service as director of the Security Assistance Division, Office of the Chief of Naval Operations; commander, Middle East Force; and deputy director for Nuclear Planning Affairs, Office of the Assistant Secretary of Defense (International Security Affairs). A 1945 graduate of the U.S. Naval Academy, he attended the Naval War College and was a research fellow in 1970-1971 at the Center for International Affairs, Harvard University.

Geoffrey Kemp, Professor of International Politics at the Fletcher School of Law and Diplomacy, Tufts University, was born in England and educated at Oxford University and M.I.T. (Ph.D., political science). Kemp is now an American citizen and has been at the Fletcher School since 1971. A prolific writer on arms transfers, defense policy and strategy for less developed countries, and Middle East military affairs, Professor Kemp, while serving as a consultant to the U.S. Senate Foreign Relations Committee, co-authored *U.S. Military Sales to Iran.* He is a consultant to the Department of Defense, Georgetown University's CSIS, the Brookings Institution, the Hudson Institute, and the Rand Corporation. He is currently completing a major study for the Twentieth Century Fund, *Implements of War: Arms Transfers and International Politics.* Other current research interests include the geopolitics of outer space.

Admiral Thomas H. Moorer, USN (Ret.) serves on the executive committee and the advisory board of CSIS. He was formerly chief of Naval Operations and chairman of the Joint Chiefs of Staff. During a distinguished career of 41 years, Admiral Moorer was the recipient of many citations and awards. He is a graduate of the U.S. Naval Academy, attended the Naval War College, and holds honorary degrees from several universities. He is the author of "Formulation of National Policy" (*Strategic Review,* Fall 1975).